In the Shadow of
the Hanging Tree

A Memoir

Katherine Baxter

Katherine Baxter

KBaxterBook@gmail.com

ISBN: 9798636654773

Cover Photo by: Katherine Baxter 1984

Printed in the United States of America

Independently Published

Philadelphia PA

For Christie and Lisa

Contents

The Majestic Oak

It's a magnificent tree. A large and majestic oak, it stands in front of the town hall, spreading its branches over the square. People rest under its shade, meet friends there, take their noonday break. The tree is a witness to lovers, family picnics, and town ceremonies.

I saw the tree on two occasions as a child and once as a teenager when my mother, father, sister and I went to family reunions in the little town of Goliad in southeast Texas. We lived in the north but kept our ties with my mother's roots in Goliad. That's where she was born, where my grandfather ran the general store, and where he and my grandmother would die.

Goliad would not be Goliad without that tree. And yet I had forgotten it during the many years since I had been to Texas. My mother was 77 and beginning to lose her memory. I had always loved hearing her tell family stories; she had agreed to tell the old favorites once more and let me tape them so they would not be lost. During one of our taping sessions, she said something about a hanging tree.

"Wait a minute, wait a minute," I said. "What do you mean, the hanging tree?"

"Oh," she said, "you know…the tree that stands in front of the town hall in Goliad. The big oak tree. That's where the Saturday night lynchings took place."

I turned off the tape recorder and stared at my mother, wondering how she could sound so casual. I had listened to her stories for many years but I had never heard about the hanging tree.

My mind went back to the Texas trip that I remembered most. It was the summer of 1939 when I was nine years old. We traveled from Maine to stay with my grandparents who lived in a sprawling white-frame house with a big porch and a big yard. On the back of the house was a storm cellar with double doors that we kids opened up when we wanted to peek inside. We tried to imagine what it would be like to see a tornado coming, and have to go into that dark scary place full of cobwebs and spiders. As a reminder that it could really happen, a huge metal rail had been ripped up from railroad tracks by the tornado of 1901, carried several miles, and deposited at a forty-five degree angle in my grandparents' yard. That piece of metal stuck so far down into the earth that no one was ever able to dislodge it, and we used it to climb on.

In Goliad, nothing was very far from anything else. I could walk about three minutes and be at the town square where I would visit my grandfather's store. Appleby's Store, it said on the front, and it sold everything. A few minutes in another direction and I could be at the farm where one of my uncles lived. We had family gatherings there, with chicken barbecued on outdoor spits and cases of soft drinks sitting under the trees to keep them cool. I was the youngest of six girl cousins. We stuck together, drinking endless bottles of Dr. Pepper, talking in Pig Latin -- a code language we were sure would confound the adults -- and trying to avoid getting kissed by too many aunts and uncles. I was awed by the four Texas cousins who were so much at home in that world. They were used to red ants and chiggers and knew how to catch horned toads. I was fascinated by the dried-up well behind my uncle's house at the farm, and kept going there to look at the snakes on the bottom. My grandmother stopped us from throwing stones at them, one of my early lessons in respect for animals.

One evening, my grandmother had a garden party at her house for the whole family, and I wore my first long dress. It was light blue. My grandmother gave me a necklace to go with it that I thought was the most beautiful thing I had ever seen, a delicate silver chain with five glass beads hanging from it -- they sparkled with soft colors and looked like diamonds. After the party, still wearing my long dress, I walked around town with my father. I glowed with the joy of staying up late and seeing the town at night.

That trip to Goliad stands out in my mind as a major life experience. Things were different there. The southern drawl. The way nobody was ever in a hurry. How everybody's name was Sugar unless you were somebody's brother, and then you were called Bubba. It all seemed a bit magical, and the garden party was the crowning event, for it made me feel grown-up and elegant. No *Gone with the Wind* fantasy of gracious living could have conjured anything more romantic in my mind.

But there were shadows too. Long, dark shadows that reached inside me and shaped the rest of my life. Race and segregation hung in the air. A white child from a white world, I wasn't used to seeing black people and I stared at them with great curiosity.

"Why do they come to the house?" I asked my mother.

"To do the laundry," she said.

"Why do they always come in the back door?"

"They're not allowed in the front door."

"Why?"

My mother sighed as she struggled to answer my questions, and to tell me that white people and black people couldn't do things together.

"But why?"

"Well, honey," she said, "it's just the way things are down here, and you can't go around asking people why."

Mother told my sister and me about a black woman who had worked for them. Her name was Caroline, but they called her Aunt Calline.

I asked her if she liked Aunt Calline.

"Yes."

"Did she come to the house a lot?"

"Yes, she did the laundry and the cooking."

"Did she eat with you?"

"No, she was not allowed to eat in the dining room; she ate in the kitchen."

It was very confusing. My mother told me that black women nursed some of the babies in our family. I didn't think anything could be closer than drinking the milk from someone else's body. Then why couldn't that woman walk in the front door of my grandmother's house and sit at her dining room table? I had been told that I should love everybody and that all people were of equal value, but that's not what I saw happening.

I have a haunting memory from that Texas visit, as clear in my mind as it was all those years ago. We had gone to visit my mother's aunt. I can still see the secluded white house, circle drive, big lawn, trees dripping with Spanish moss. It was not a large house but it seemed elegant to me, and remains in my mind as stereotypically southern.

What caught my attention was a round white gazebo in the front yard. Inside was an old black woman, tall and dark skinned, sitting very still, her head bent over her work. She was surrounded by piles of clothes that she seemed to be mending.

"Who is that?" I asked.

My great-aunt replied, "Oh her, that's Lackey."

"What is she doing there?"

"She's one of our servants. She's been with our family for years. Now she's old and not right in the head, but we keep her on and give her easy work to do."

My next question was cut off before I could finish it; I was to get no more information about Lackey. The adults moved to the front porch of the house and sat on rocking chairs while my great-aunt served iced coffee. I paid little attention to them, for my mind was on the gazebo. I knew with all my heart that what I saw was not right. The gazebo looked like a cage. Lackey was the prisoner and that's the way black people were treated. I wanted to let Lackey out of the cage and make everything all right, but all I could do was feel sad. Nobody seemed to notice me; they sat on the porch for the longest time, rocking and talking and sipping iced coffee.

For years afterwards, I would dream about the gazebo. From time to time, there it would come, that memory of Goliad. I would see myself as a child once more, standing on the circle drive, looking at Lackey and longing to set her free.

One day in Goliad, I overheard my mother telling my father how prejudiced her younger brother was. That was my uncle who lived on the farm. My mother said she was worried about the way he was bringing up his son, afraid that he would be prejudiced too. After that, I was afraid of my uncle; I looked at him with great curiosity but I stayed away from him.

That was the first time I remember knowing that my parents were concerned about issues of race. Because of them, my own awareness began at an early age but it was vague and jumbled. With great amusement, my parents used to tell a story about me when I was three and we had gone out to dinner at a small family-style restaurant. Sitting in my high chair, I leaned over to the people at the next table and announced in a loud voice, "My Daddy was a nigger when he was a little boy."

Nobody could figure out where that came from, especially since my parents never used that word. However, the summer I was nine, my views about race began to take on more reality. It was only in Goliad that I saw black people, and it was there that I experienced the world as broken. On one side were black people who were treated badly. On the other side were white people who didn't seem to know that anything was wrong. I learned two rules that summer: you weren't supposed to ask questions and you had to stay on your own side of the world.

When I was taping my mother's stories, it brought back those Texas memories. I asked her to tell me about the hanging tree. She said that when someone was sentenced to death, he was taken directly from the courthouse to the tree, and hung. She thought that was pretty gruesome, but it was the lynchings that gave her the most painful memories. When she was a child, sometimes on a Saturday afternoon, white men would ride up to the house on horseback, shouting "Keep the kids in tonight! There's gonna be a lynching, the niggers are getting uppity." Then they would ride off.

My mother thought it was the Klan that did the lynchings, and she suspected that her younger brother had been a member of the Klan, though she didn't know for sure. No one ever talked about it. She only hoped he had never been part of a lynch mob.

As a child, she had tried to ask questions about why black people weren't treated the same as whites but she had always been slapped down for it. That was her term: "slapped down." It was true even after she left home. When she was about thirty and went to Goliad to visit her family, she decided to be defiant by setting the dining room table for enough people to include the black servant. My grandmother was furious, and ordered her never to do such a thing again. Mother removed the extra place setting and kept her silence about how she felt. All her life, she harbored a hatred of segregation and the pain and cruelty it caused. As an old woman, she would weep when she talked about those times. "It was so terrible," she said, "it was so terrible."

My mother's stories are deeply imbedded in me. So are my own memories of Goliad. The hanging tree too, for it seems to me now that I have always lived in its shadow. It has become a grim reminder of the things I struggled to understand that summer in Goliad. That's where my heart began to ache for the broken world and where I first knew that I wanted to put it back together.

Crossing the Line

In 1947, with my family now living in Chicago, I became a student at Grinnell College in Iowa. In the fall semester of my sophomore year, the school announced that it was going to take part in an exchange program with Hampton Institute, an all-black college in Virginia. Three students from Grinnell would be selected to go to Hampton for the spring semester and three students from Hampton would come to Grinnell. Oberlin College was also participating in the program; a total of six white students would be at Hampton that semester. I was excited when I read the notice. It was as though a door had opened and someone had finally invited me to explore the issues I most cared about. Not many students applied, but I held my breath until the selections were made.

I was thrilled when I learned that I had been chosen, and I was sure my parents would be excited too. But when I called to tell them, there was silence on the other end of the line. My heart sank when I heard my parents fumbling for a response. With shock and disbelief, I realized that they didn't want me to go.

For days afterward, I felt the pain of betrayal, and I didn't understand it. My parents were ardent lefties. They supported Franklin Delano Roosevelt, labor unions, and many left wing causes. My father took me to Hull House because he wanted me to know about its founder, Jane Addams, the 19th century reformer. He took my sister and me to Soldiers Field in Chicago to hear FDR. He took us to hear Henry Wallace, presidential candidate for the Progressive Party.

Most memorable of all, he introduced us to Paul Robeson. I don't know how he did it, but he arranged an evening for about a dozen teenagers from our church to meet with Robeson. I knew him as a singer, his Ballad for Americans a beloved 78 rpm recording my friend Mary and I knew by heart when we were nine years old. (I still have it.) But now I had the opportunity to sit in a circle with Robeson as he talked about his life and opened my eyes to racism in a way I had never known.

My parents cared a lot about racism. They hated what they had seen of it in the south, and they wanted us to care, too. But they didn't want me to go to Hampton.

In the weeks that followed my phone call, they tried to discourage me from taking part in the exchange program. I had no intention of changing my plans, but their long faces took the edge off my excitement. Looking back, I imagine that my parents were frightened for me. What a difference it might have made if they had talked about it. And, for that matter, if I could have expressed what it meant to me to have this opportunity. But we were not accustomed to that kind of sharing. At the time, I felt only a numbed sense of abandonment. It was as though my parents had set boundaries to the support they would give me. I had crossed the line and they were no longer there to cheer me on.

It was February when I boarded the train, a month before my nineteenth birthday. I went with two male students who were also taking part in the exchange program. We changed trains at Washington, D.C. which was the dividing line on the railroads between North and South. From there, we rode in a segregated train, traveling in a car for whites only. When we arrived at Hampton, several people met us at the station, including Willa who would be my roommate. She was a senior, knew everybody, was helpful and patient, good humored and fun. She took me under her wing and helped me through the ropes as I settled into campus life; I thought she was wonderful. The hurts and disappointments of my family's reactions were set aside as I jumped full-swing into my new adventure.

There were cultural differences that were immediately apparent. One was the food. Having Texas parents, I had grown up with southern cooking as part of my diet, but I never knew anyone who ate biscuits and yams and greens every day. We did at Hampton -- I didn't see a white potato the entire semester. Sweet potato pie was new to me, and I loved it. I ate on the early dinner shift to be sure I got there before the sweet potato pie was gone.

I came to love Duke Ellington and Billy Eckstine, their music always coming from someone's room in the dormitory. I learned to dance the hucklebuck, though not with the skill of the students who could create the most amazing variations. All of that felt like an integral part of Hampton. If you didn't like the Duke or Billy or dance the hucklebuck, what were you doing there?

One of the biggest surprises was how well the students dressed. At Grinnell I was used to casual clothing, but Hampton women wore dresses and stockings. I upgraded my own clothing pretty quickly.

Students did not go off campus nearly as much as I was used to doing. A full social life was provided on campus because going to town meant having to deal with segregation. Dark-skinned foreigners were served in local restaurants where U.S. blacks were not allowed. There were stories of black Americans who went into a restaurant, put on a foreign accent, and got served. Students laughed when they told those stories, but they were bitter. For them, town was a hostile place. Nevertheless, they did go occasionally. I made a trip with Willa soon after I got there. I told her I was not going to ride in the front of the bus while she sat in the back, but she sternly told me that's exactly what I *was* going to do. So on the way in, I rode up front. We walked around town and bought a few things without incident except for people staring at us. Seeing a black person and a white person together as friends was an extraordinary event in those days in Virginia. In one store the clerk sold us cigarettes as though nothing was unusual, but when we asked for matches she only stared at us. Willa politely asked her again but the woman continued to stare. On the third request, the clerk shook herself as though coming out of a trance, and gave us some matches.

Before we started back, I told Willa I could not sit in the front of the bus again. I knew this was not a simple matter and I didn't want to make trouble for her, but I couldn't do it. When I told her I'd walk back if necessary, she relented and we sat together. Nobody gave us a hard time, they just looked at us in disbelief. One white woman leaned so far out of her seat to stare at us that she lost her balance and nearly fell into the aisle. Willa and I kept straight faces until we got safely back to campus. I had heard of passing only in terms of black people passing for white, but now I knew that passing was something I could do too. The two or three times that I went into town with Willa again, nothing more happened than people staring as we sat together in the back of the bus.

Color was an uncomfortable subject for most white people I knew, but at Hampton, it was a fact of life and did not cause embarrassment. People talked about it with ease, and they teased me for sitting in the sun. "You trying to look like us?" they asked. They explained the color hierarchy on campus, pointing out that the light-skinned students had higher status. They were simply giving me information, telling me things they thought I should know.

I soon became friendly with Emma, who lived on my floor of the dorm. One day she took me to the beauty parlor that was in the basement. A number of students were there, having their hair straightened. The scene took my breath away. I knew that black women had their hair straightened, for I had never seen any with their hair in its natural state. But to see it happening in that dark basement, out of sight, was eerie. I stood and stared, feeling a sudden sharp awareness of what black people went through to try to measure up to white norms.

Color differences also had their funnier moments. When Emma showed me the laundry room, she watched for a few minutes as I ironed a blouse. Then she pushed me away and proceeded to do the fastest and most beautiful ironing I'd ever seen. "What you were doing wouldn't pass kindergarten," she said. "White folks never did learn how to iron properly."

I joined a modern dance group at Hampton. There I learned about Harriet Tubman, the black woman who escaped from slavery and went back to the south 19 times to lead others to freedom. We did a dance about her in which I was one of the slaves. That was my first taste of African American history. We went on tour several times in North Carolina, South Carolina, and Georgia. At first it seemed like a lark. We got out of classes, performed for appreciative audiences, and were often entertained afterwards by our hosts. Sometimes we went out on our own to a nightclub. But I soon learned there was much more to it than having a good time. The dance group gave me an education I never could have gotten in a classroom.

One of the first things I learned was what it was like for black people to travel in the south. The organizers of our tours had to make careful plans because we could not use hotels and other public facilities. Most of the time, we stayed in private homes and rode in charter buses. Still, there was no getting away from Jim Crow. The places where we stopped for rest rooms and food showed me first-hand that Separate but Equal was always separate but never equal. For black bus passengers, it meant going into a tiny building, often no more than a shack, with a sign that said Colored. Next to it would be a large well-kept building with a sign reading For Whites Only.

Once, in North Carolina, we squeezed into the little building for Colored, wanting to get drinks to go with our lunch. We bought milk, which was the only thing available, but there were no straws. It got very quiet and everyone was looking at me. "Oh no," I said, when I realized what they were thinking. "Oh, yes," was their response, "it's no big deal." They wanted me to go to the white building to get straws.

I took a deep breath when I went inside. The lunch counter was at the back, which meant that I had to walk the entire length of the bus station to get there. At least the place was busy, full of people talking; I thought I wouldn't be noticed. But before I got halfway through the building, it became strangely quiet. As I looked cautiously around, I saw that everyone was watching me. All talking had stopped. There was no sound except my footsteps.

I made it to the lunch counter and got the straws. Keeping my eyes straight ahead, I tried to get out of there as fast as I could. Just as I got to the door, a woman approached me. "Excuse me," she said, "but people saw you coming from the building for Colored and there's a bet going on as to whether you are white or black. Would you mind telling me?" I was about to give her a flip answer and beat a hasty retreat but I saw that she was friendly, so I told her what I was doing. We talked for a few minutes, then she thanked me and wished me well. I turned and saw that everyone was on the bus waiting for me, with anxious faces pressed to the windows. We made jokes about what happened next in the bus station, who won and who lost the bet, and what they said about me. I was happy to be out of there.

On another trip, we went to Atlanta. This time we rode by train and stayed in dormitories at Morehouse and Spelman colleges. Some of our hosts were to meet us at the train station. It was more than a courtesy, it was a safety precaution as well. Each southern city had its own prohibitions for black people, and if you didn't know what to expect, it could mean trouble. In one city you could take any kind of cab, in another you'd better look only for cabs driven by blacks. In one city you could ride the bus without trouble, in another you couldn't. If you were new to an area, it wasn't a good idea to strike out on your own without knowing the unwritten rules.

When we arrived in Atlanta our hosts were not there yet, so we stayed at the train station in the waiting room that was designated for Colored. Before long, a white policeman asked me to move to the white section. When I told him I was where I belonged, his mouth dropped open and he stared at me. He stammered a few incoherent words, turned red, and left. Not wanting any further encounters like that, I went to the ladies' room and stayed there until our hosts arrived. From then on I was known as the girl who hides in ladies' rooms.

Our dance instructor was a white woman, and I was the only white student. We were the first integrated group to perform at the civic auditorium in Atlanta. After our performance that night, a number of us went to a nightclub. An hour or so later, I went upstairs with several others to play the slot machines. When we came down again, we discovered that everybody else in our group had left. We thought it was strange but decided to go back to the dorms.

The next morning I learned why the others had left the nightclub without us. They assumed that I had already gone, and were worried about my safety. With visions of this innocent white woman roaming around lost in the black part of Atlanta, not knowing the rules of the game, they spent a couple of hours looking for me. I was extraordinarily moved by that. There I was, the one who had the most freedom of movement, sleeping peacefully while they were worrying about me.

On the way back from Atlanta, I ate in a Jim Crow dining car for the first time. We sat in the Colored section, a small area behind a curtain that separated us from the large area for white diners. I felt horrible about the experience. It was so insulting, so humiliating. But during that meal I was reminded about the use of humor as a survival skill. When we were served vanilla ice cream for dessert, several students held handkerchiefs over their dishes, trying to hide the ice cream. They took surreptitious bites, cracked jokes, talked in stage whispers, and looked furtively around as though they would be arrested if they were caught eating something white.

That night I stayed up late and went into the lounge car of the white section to get a sandwich. A few minutes later, a man sat down next to me. We started talking, but he began to get friendlier than I wanted. When he asked me where I was going, I told him I was the only white member of a group of black dancers and we were on tour. Then I turned my head for a moment. When I turned back again, he was gone. He just disappeared! I thought to myself: Well, that's a new one. Now I know how to get rid of unwanted advances from a white man.

I went back to the Jim Crow car and sat with the older man who did the stage lighting for our performances. Leon must have been about 40. He had grown up on a small farm and only now had the chance to go to college. We became engrossed in conversation as we talked about our lives. After awhile he told me this was the first time he had ever talked with a white person as an equal. Suddenly we were silent. I had enjoyed our sharing, the two of us late at night, speaking from our hearts. We didn't have to play the role of student or white person or black person or older person or teenager; all the boundaries were gone. So much of our interaction on the tour had been with the group, joking and laughing, calling back and forth to one another. Now, with everyone else asleep, it was a time set apart, with nothing outside of ourselves except the noise of the train speeding along somewhere in Georgia.

We were at ease with one another, simply being ourselves. Leon's words about this being a first-time experience suddenly made it extraordinary. It brought us back to who and where we were and silenced us with the weight of what that meant. As I sat there, taking in what had happened, I thought how hard it was to cross the color line. Yet it was possible. Leon and I both felt that...how amazing it was to have made this contact.

When I was on campus, I started dating a young black man from New York state. He was at Hampton because he had never experienced discrimination and he felt isolated from the black community. He wanted to know what life was like for other black people. I enjoyed his company but I felt no particular attraction.

And then I met Larry. He was a tall, dark-skinned handsome man who made my heart skip a beat. I scarcely knew him when I saw him one day, walking with two other students. I watched them pass, then called, "Hi,

Larry." He turned around, paused, then returned the greeting. His friends gave him understanding smiles. After that, we began spending time together.

Having a love affair was not something I had looked for. But, like the dance group, it was an experience that taught me things I would not have learned in a classroom. For example, a student passed me one day and said mockingly, "Hello, Miss Ann." When I asked Larry what it meant, he was angry that it had happened. He said Miss Ann was a term for a white woman who is having an affair with her black chauffeur or butler.

One day we decided to go to town for a movie. I thought it was risky, particularly for him, but he was sure we could get away with it. It was tempting because we wanted to do normal things together. We did get away with it but it certainly did not feel normal. First, we went to a small black-run eating place and had ice cream which I didn't enjoy because I was so nervous. Then I went to the theater by myself, bought a ticket and found a seat. When the movie began, Larry came in and sat beside me. We held hands in the dark but by the time I began to relax, the movie was over and we had to pretend we didn't know each other. We left the theater separately and met a couple of blocks away where friends picked us up and drove us back to the school.

Staying on campus had its own difficulties, particularly in finding a place to be alone. Once, we thought we had finally found a nice spot for some private kissing, only to be chased away by a campus security guard. Another time, Larry had been grounded and we hadn't been together for almost a week. I walked by his dorm one day and saw him leaning out the window. "Your chemistry teacher is looking for you," I lied. We went to the science building by different routes and had five passionate minutes on a secluded stairway.

By then, I was in turmoil. Hampton was a very emotional experience, even without Larry. It was painful to look so closely at segregation and get a feel for what it meant to people who had to live with it every day. I was keenly aware that I could walk away from it and they could not. I treasured what I was learning and was moved that my friends were so accepting of me. I was inspired by them. In the midst of a hostile environment, the students I met had great strength and dignity and humor. And for the first time, I was surrounded by people who cared about the same social issues that I did. Nobody evaded questions or acted embarrassed or picked arguments with me. At

Hampton I felt at home. Yet of course it wasn't my home. In a few weeks I would be back in the white world where my opinions and feelings about race would not be counted for much.

There was no opportunity to talk about any of these things. I rarely saw the other exchange students and I had no contact with anyone at Grinnell. No one had prepared me for what I might encounter at Hampton, and I had no faculty advisor who kept in touch with me after I was there.

Hampton seemed like a setup for white women to fall in love with black men. It happened not just to me that semester but to the two women from Oberlin, as well. The white men did not have love affairs but the women did. We learned that the same thing had happened the previous year, when two other white colleges had participated in the exchange program.

The year I was there, one of the women from Oberlin broke her engagement to a man back in Ohio because of her love affair at Hampton. On our last day there, she and her Hampton friend went out to lunch with Larry and me. It was a gloomy meal. Larry and I had decided there could be no future for us, and we were saying goodbye. The following day, on the trip home, some of my friends were on the same train, but I rode alone most of the time and cried. It was my last ride in a Jim Crow car. At Washington we changed trains. There we parted, I going to my world, the Hampton students to theirs. We knew we would not see each other again.

When I got home, I showed Larry's picture to my parents. My mother's only comment was, "He certainly is Negroid, isn't he?" I didn't expect to get much sympathy for this love affair, but her response made it clear that I would have none at all. I felt no support from either my father or my mother for anything about my Hampton experience. I was bursting to talk about what I had seen and done and learned but they didn't want to hear about it. They acted as though nothing had happened. When I visited my mother's best friend and she asked about Hampton, I talked at length, happy that someone was interested. Then she said, "I suppose you got used to the odor after awhile." I stared at her, trying to figure out what she meant. "The smell of colored people," she said. My heart seemed to stop, for I did not know how to answer such an appalling comment. But Ruth," I replied, "nobody…" but she wasn't listening. Neither of us had anything more to say.

Every once in awhile that summer, I went to a quiet part of the house and cried. My mother found me once, and looked at me with an expression of great sorrow but, without a word, she turned and walked away. I never doubted that my mother loved me but, like her own mother, she seemed unable to put into words the most personal and emotional parts of herself, or to help me express mine.

It was my friend Sylvia who kept me from feeling completely alone with my experience. She and I met occasionally at a local park where she listened to my stories of Hampton and Larry and provided tissues for drying my tears. Sometimes I went to her home where, in the tradition of her Russian parents, we sat at the kitchen table and sipped hot tea from glasses as we talked about our lives. Our friendship eased the pain of the silence I experienced at home.

Later that year, I heard from Larry and we began a correspondence that lasted until the following summer. When he came to visit me in Chicago, we spent a day together and talked about getting married. But not long after that, I ended the relationship. I did not have the courage to stand in that much opposition to my family.

The emotional turmoil that was part of my Hampton experience did not dampen my appreciation for what it had given me. I ached for my parents to know how privileged I felt for having taken part in the student exchange. But no matter what I said, they seemed to hate it. Especially my mother. She was bitterly resentful, as though because of that program, she had lost her daughter. To some extent she had, for I had crossed a line and moved into territory that she could not accept. For 20 years it would lie between us, a source of tension and hurt we did not know how to heal.

And then one day, the ground quietly shifted. I was visiting my mother not long after my father died. I hadn't planned to bring the subject up, but as my mother and I were having a leisurely, cozy kind of conversation, it suddenly came tumbling out, once again telling her how precious my Hampton experience was to me. Tears filled my mother's eyes and she nodded her head. She didn't say a word, but I knew she was telling me that she understood. It was all I needed to know. It was like feeling that I could breathe again, that old wounds were healed, old tensions and hurts finally put to rest.

What Color Am I?

I've never known why Grinnell College took part in the exchange program. The three of us who participated were given no support while we were at Hampton, and there was barely any follow-up when we returned. One evening we talked about our experiences to a small group of students and faculty, but there was nothing more. I felt tremendously let down.

At the end of the fall term, I transferred to Roosevelt College (now Roosevelt University) in Chicago, an easy commute from home. I had heard about this school, one of the first in the country that did not ask its applicants about their race, religion, or nationality. Seeking diversity in its outlook, it attracted teachers who left other schools and came to Roosevelt, often at a lower salary, because of the freedom of speech they enjoyed there.

The school was housed in the former Auditorium Hotel on Michigan Boulevard, overlooking Grant Park and Lake Michigan. When I enrolled in 1950, the building was no longer the beauty it had once been; the wooden floors were worn and creaky and paint was peeling from the walls. But the school was thriving with interesting events in addition to formal classes: impromptu jazz sessions, guest speakers, discussion groups. The atmosphere was exhilarating. I loved walking through the halls of that seedy old building and hearing bits of conversations from students of every shade of skin color and the whole spectrum of religious and political beliefs. There was no question that this was the place for me.

I graduated in 1951, and became an elementary school teacher in the Chicago public schools. Soon after, I met Bruce Baxter at the Unitarian church where my father was the minister. We married in 1956, and two years later, Lisa was born. I took a six-month maternity leave, then returned to the classroom, assigned to an elementary school in a black community.

I had previously taught in another black community. My best friend there had been a white woman. Anita and I ate lunch together and often shared rides to school. One day she told me that one of the black teachers had asked her to find out if I was white or black. Anita assumed that I was white, but she told Lorraine she didn't know for sure. I was astonished by the question. I told Lorraine I was white, and we had a good laugh about it. I dismissed the incident, sure it was something that would never happen again.

Now, a year later, I was in a school where there was hostility between black and white faculty members. In order to avoid each other, white teachers ate in the cafeteria and black teachers ate in the faculty lounge. Brenda soon became my best friend at the school. Because she was black, I ate lunch with her in the lounge.

I was in the auditorium one day, watching children rehearse for a program, when Brenda came in and sat beside me. Looking troubled, she told me we couldn't be seen together anymore because "there's a rumor going around school that you are trying to pass for white." I couldn't take in this crazy thing she had said. Maybe she meant that people thought I was trying to pass for black.

She could no longer keep from laughing. "You heard me right," she said, "at least the part about the rumor. People think you are trying to pass for white."

"But that doesn't make sense," I said, "If I were trying to pass, why would I hang out with you? I'd go over to the cafeteria and eat with the white teachers."

Brenda threw up her hands. "You're asking me to figure this out? But while you're trying to decide what color you want to be, I hope you'll still have lunch with me."

When I observed more closely, I saw how rigid the color line was. Not only did teachers eat in different places, they visited in groups in the halls by color and even duplicated classroom materials on different machines. In a faculty of over 80 people, apparently I was the only one who crossed the line. From my first day on the job, I came and went as I pleased, was friendly with white teachers as well as black, and used whatever machine I felt like for duplicating materials (though I never saw the lunch room.) No wonder people were confused about my identity. Savoring the unique position I was in, I decided to keep everyone guessing.

I began to notice a difference in the way people behaved toward me. Even Brenda. She was still friendly, but she seemed to keep a slight distance. I guessed that while she had originally assumed I was white, she was now unsure.

One day, when I was walking in an isolated part of the basement, I was approached by three black teachers. One of them was Brenda, and one was Althea, the woman I rode to school with every day. They gave me a friendly greeting, but blocked my path. One of them said, "O.K., Kathy, let's have it. What are you?" I laughed and said, "Maybe I'm Indian." I moved around them and continued on my way.

I felt bad about not telling Brenda and Althea, but I was intrigued by what was happening. Without realizing it, I had broken a taboo and I wanted to see how long I could get away with it. I was also learning something about the labels we put on people. Since no one at the school was sure what my label was, they couldn't tell if I was one of "us" or one of "them." As a result, they didn't seem to know what to do with me. Perhaps I couldn't have kept it up very long, but for the time being, I liked being able to connect with both worlds without having to choose one over the other.

After one semester, I transferred to a school closer to home where I lived with a white identity. I treasured the memory of that brief time when no one knew my color, and I couldn't help laughing when I thought about it. But I had a new life now. I was absorbed with caring for Lisa, teaching, and providing support for Bruce who was finishing his studies at the University of Chicago. In 1959, when Lisa was a year and a half, he received his Ph.D. and began a career in pharmaceutical research. His first job was at the University of California Medical School in San Francisco.

Old Dreams

We rented a pink house in the Sunset District of San Francisco, with the zoo a couple of blocks away in one direction, the ocean a couple of blocks in another. We could open our back windows and hear the lions roaring and the gibbons whooping. We could lean out the front window and watch the sunset. Bruce and I were charmed with San Francisco. But I needed to get a teaching job in order to supplement our income, and the one I found was on the other side of the Golden Gate Bridge. And so we moved again, this time to Corte Madera.

That school year of 1960-61, I taught fourth grade. The U.S. history textbook I used began with early European explorers and went up to the present time. A few months into the term, I began to feel that something was wrong. When we came to the subject of slavery, it dawned on me what the problem was, for this huge issue was barely mentioned and only in the most superficial way. Throughout the rest of the book, there was hardly a clue that black people existed. The history I was teaching was lily-white.

I strongly believed that this was not real history at all, only a cleaned-up mythical version. It was bad for black children who could not see themselves in those pages, and bad for white children too, for it deprived them of an honest view of American life. I resolved that as soon as I could, I would look for materials that would paint a fuller picture. I hadn't forgotten my old dreams of building bridges between black and white. Here was a tangible way that I could do something about it.

It took a few more years before that would happen, and two more moves. The first was to Evansville, Indiana in 1961 where Bruce had a new job and where Christie, our second daughter, was born.

In Evansville, I became a member of the Mayor's Commission on Human Relations. In that capacity, I joined a committee to study the segregated housing patterns in Evansville. The following year, I read an article about fair housing councils, groups of people who challenged segregation in their own communities. I was excited about the prospect of starting such a group in Evansville but by then, Bruce had taken another job. And so, after three years in Evansville, we prepared for another move. I hated to abandon my plans for a fair housing council. Little did I know that I was moving to a place where one already existed.

From Black to White

Before we left Indiana, we called the office of a large apartment complex in King of Prussia, a Philadelphia suburb not far from where Bruce would be working. The woman we spoke to said there was a vacancy, so we filled out the forms, had our credit checked, and made a deposit. But she would not send us a lease; she said the manager needed to see both husband and wife in person before the papers were signed. Bruce and I were puzzled but when we got there and did not see any people of color in the entire development, we decided the manager wanted to make sure both of us were white.

A few days after we moved in, I was surprised to see a black child get off the school bus and head toward one of the apartments. I followed him, noted where he lived, and the next day I went and introduced myself to his mother. Jane invited me in, told me that she and her husband and two sons were the only African Americans living in the apartment complex, and that she was a member of the

Upper Merion Fair Housing Council. The council had helped her family get an apartment by proving that the manager had lied when he told them there were no vacancies. When white members of the council checked and found that there were actually quite a few vacancies, they confronted the manager who then backed down and rented an apartment to Jane's family. Two weeks after I arrived in King of Prussia, Jane took me to a meeting of the Upper Merion Fair Housing Council. It was exactly what I had envisioned when I was in Evansville. By the time I left the meeting that evening, I was an active member, having already taken part in making decisions about future actions.

The council was bi-racial. It was started by whites, but blacks joined as they moved into the area. We gave support to every black family coming into the community, and did our best to outwit sellers and realtors who were trying to keep King of Prussia white. They tried to outwit us too; "For Sale" signs no longer appeared on front lawns. But we found out which houses were on the market, and we kept families informed, largely with the help of council members who had ties to black communities.

I worried about the impact my involvement with the fair housing council was having on Lisa and Christie. I was often on the phone, sometimes went out to check the availability of a house or apartment, and went to meetings almost every week. Christie was three when we moved to King of Prussia. She was in pre-school part of the time. Lisa was six and in first grade. I loved spending time with my girls, and felt like an inadequate mother for not spending more. When I was particularly busy with the council, I consoled myself with the thought that I was helping create a better world for my daughters to live in.

I was inspired by the Civil Rights Movement. I followed events avidly, went to discussion groups and workshops on nonviolence, and took part in demonstrations. We were optimistic in those days. With "White Only" signs coming down from many public facilities, and schools being desegregated, we saw housing as the last bastion. I believed it was possible that in my lifetime the color barrier in this country would become a thing of the past. I don't remember when I was jolted out of that belief. I only know that by the late '60s, I saw that as knowledgeable and progressive as I felt myself to be, I was woefully ignorant about the depth of racism in this country.

Not long after I joined the fair housing council, Jane, who had introduced me to the council, asked if I had read

Before the Mayflower by Lerone Bennett. She was so excited about the book that I purchased a copy and to my surprise, found that I was reading African American history. I was awed by *Before the Mayflower*. On every page I found evidence that black people were part and parcel of the whole sweep of U.S. history.

I was thirty-five when I discovered this history. It was like unlocking the door to a secret closet and finding stories that had been kept from me. After *Before the Mayflower*, I read books by historians John Hope Franklin, Benjamin Quarles, W.E.B. DuBois, and others. I read poetry and novels by black writers, took a course in African American history, watched black films, and went twice to Washington, D.C. to attend the annual three-day convention of the Association for the Study of Negro Life and History (in 1972, it was changed to African American.)

I was moved by the stories I found, especially the biographies. They made me realize that my education had supported the myth that black people were weak and submissive. What different images I was now getting! People like Mary McLeod Bethune who started a school in Florida for black children and stood up to the Klan when they tried to burn it down. Here was not the black woman of my childhood dream, Lackey with a bowed head, sitting in a gazebo. I cried when I read the story of Mary McLeod Bethune, not for sorrow, but for her strength and dignity, her quiet courage, her head held high.

I also read stories of white people. I began to think that they, too, had been portrayed as weak and submissive, because it seemed as though they rarely questioned the way things were. The only white person I knew about who had challenged slavery was John Brown, but he was thought to be a great exception and half crazy. Now I learned about James and Lucretia Mott, Charlotte and Sarah Grimke, and other white people who challenged slavery and white supremacy. How wonderful to find these additions to all the white male heroes I was supposed to idolize.

It was in 1965 that I read *Before the Mayflower*, not many months after the march from Selma, Alabama to Montgomery, a march to end the practices that made it impossible for black people to vote or even register to vote.

When I saw photographs of black people being shoved and bullied and beaten, I was stunned by the hate-filled faces of white people. It was the same hate I had seen in the pictures of white people in Arkansas eight years earlier when the first black students were ushered into the high school in Little Rock. The same hate, a few years after that, in the faces of white people in Greensboro, North Carolina as they taunted and jabbed and dumped food over the heads of black students sitting-in at an all-white lunch counter in Woolworth's.

In the 50s, when I saw the photographs from Little Rock and Greensboro, I felt indignation and disgust for the white people who were so hostile. But after Selma, when I was soaking up black history and reading biographies, I looked at pictures of young white people with distorted faces, mouths wide open to spew out obscenities, hands lifted to throw bricks, and I felt tremendous sorrow. For in the faces of those people, so afraid of the way their world was changing, I saw only hate and rage. There was no sign of love or hope or dreams. I was coming to understand what James Baldwin meant when he said that black folks lose their lives and white folks lose their souls.

About a year after Selma, I read *Killers of the Dream* by Lillian Smith, a white southern writer and advocate for racial justice. Her views were similar to Baldwin's, for she believed that segregation damaged the souls of white folks. "They learn to pray at night," she said, "and ride Jim Crow cars the next morning, to believe in democracy and practice slavery, to be gentle people and arrogant callous creatures in the same moment."

A member of the club that Lillian's mother belonged to had discovered a little white girl in the colored part of town, living with a black family in what was described as hardly more than a pigsty. The next day, the clubwomen, escorted by the town marshal, took the child away from the family, despite their protestations and their tears. Janie was taken to Lillian's home where the two children soon became friends. They ate together, played together, read Bible verses together, and soon "a deeply felt bond grew up between us."

But the time came when the clubwomen learned that Janie really was a black child. After whispered meetings with other adults, Lillian's mother told her that Janie would be returned to Colored Town.

"But why?"

"Because she's a colored girl; she can't live with whites."

"But she's white!"

"We were mistaken. She is colored."

"But she looks…"

"She is colored. Please don't argue!"

"Can she come to play?"

"No."

"I don't understand."

"You're too young to understand. And don't ask me again, ever again, about this!"

Thirty years later, as a nine-year-old child in Goliad, I would ask the same kinds of questions. No matter how my mother felt, there was nothing else she could do but give the same kinds of answers.

Lillian Smith was the first white person I knew of who shared my heartache about black and white. Yes, I kept saying as I read. Yes, this is it, this is what I mean. In 1949, when I went to Hampton, she had already put into words what I was just beginning to know: that in the process of damaging black people, white people damage themselves. We are the killers of our own dreams.

I thought about the way I had taught American history to my fourth grade students in California. I had denied those children the knowledge that had been denied to me. I had kept closed those secret doors that locked out other people and other ideas. When I left California in 1961, I promised myself that I would find materials that would keep me from teaching that way again. Several years later, I began looking for children's books that contained positive images of black people, that portrayed white people who fought slavery and segregation, and that told the stories of

Black history. I would take those books with me when I went back to the classroom.

I continued to be active with the fair housing council because I wanted to be part of the struggle for equal opportunity. But I no longer thought it was only black people who needed change. As I put more time and passion into the search for school materials, I began to shift my focus from black to white. Black children needed the books I was looking for. Yes, I knew that. They needed them for a sense of visibility and self-worth. But I wanted those books for white children, too. I wanted to unlock the secret doors that would help them open their hearts and minds.

Sharing the Stories

Wanting to start a library with the books I was collecting, I had my eye on a small storefront building in Ardmore, a town along Philadelphia's Main Line. The space was being used as an office by the Main Line Fair Housing Council. I knew the people and I thought the location might be ideal. The library could serve the black community and also be a resource for local schools, thus serving the white community as well. The office was crowded but I was given a corner by the front window. I set up a book shelf, brought over a dozen storybooks that depicted black children, and put a sign in the window inviting people to browse. The following day two little black girls came in on their way home from school. I greeted them and they sat down on the floor and began looking at the books. In a couple of minutes, one of the girls began to beam. "Look," she said to her friend, "the children in this book are the same color as us!" The second girl moved over closer and they read the book together, oblivious to everything around them. The library was in business.

I recruited several friends, we created a board of directors, raised some money, and bought more books. When the fair housing council moved out, we took over the whole space and gave ourselves a name: Gate Library. It was wonderful to see the excitement of the black children as they saw themselves reflected in these books, but I was eager to reach white children as well. I wanted to go into schools to encourage teachers to use the library as a classroom resource. No one else on the board seemed interested, but I hoped I could persuade them. I saw no conflict in serving all of the nearby communities.

One of the directors was Jeanne, a black woman I liked and admired, but she disagreed with me about the goals of the library. One evening at a board meeting in my home, she stated emphatically that the library was not there to serve the white community and that had never been the intention of the founders. I was furious. I was the one who got the space and put those first books in the window and opened the library. "The goals may have changed," I said, "but don't tell me what they were at the beginning because I was the beginning!"

Jeanne got up and put her coat on, ready to walk out. I said, "Just a minute. You decide right now if you intend to stay on the board or if you're going to leave." She looked startled, then said that she was leaving the board. Jeanne walked out, and there was silence in the room. No one had seen me explode before; they had known only the Kathy who was patient and soft-spoken.

My belief in the need to serve the white community was supported by the slave narratives I was reading. During the 1970s, I made numerous trips to the Library Company in Philadelphia and the Schomburg Library in Harlem, eventually reading 32 of these books in the original. Slave narratives are accounts of the authors' experiences in slavery and their eventual escape, often told to someone who wrote them down and made them into books. Many of the former slaves went on speaking tours and sold their books, raising money so they could buy wives, husbands, and children out of slavery. They are powerful stories. Moving, heartbreaking, inspiring. I was also struck that from time to time, they included comments about the effects that slavery had on the master. "Under the influence of slavery's polluting power," wrote Henry Box Brown who had escaped from Virginia, "the most gentle women become the fiercest viragos, and the most benevolent men are changed into inhuman monsters."

This view was echoed by Frederick Douglass who wrote about his life with the Auld family in Baltimore where he had been sent as a child. He described Mrs. Auld as a pious, warm, and tender-hearted woman. Seeing that Frederick was bright, Mrs. Auld began teaching him to read. But when her husband discovered what she was doing, he ordered her to stop, saying that it was strictly forbidden to teach slaves to read. After that, Douglass wrote, slavery proved its ability to divest her of her heavenly qualities. "Under its influence, the tender heart became stone, and the lamb-like disposition gave way to one of tiger-like fierceness."

Occasionally there were comments about differences between slave states and free states. John Brown, who had escaped from Georgia, said that "poor whites are worse off in the Slave States than they ever can be in the Free States, because in the Slave States labour is made shameful, and a man does not like to go to his own fields for fear folks should look down upon him."
What more needs to be said about the damage that slavery and white supremacy do to white people?

After I exploded at the board meeting that evening at my house, we carried on with the business at hand, but I knew it was the beginning of the end for me. How can it be, I had asked, that it is not important to offer the services of Gate Library to the communities that lie all around us, both black and white? Why isn't there more concern for white people's ignorance about slavery and racism? But Jeanne was not the only one to dismiss my views. A white woman who had recently come to work with the library was even more vehement in her opposition. While I did not feel resistance from others, neither did I have an ally. Gate Library was thriving, and it served a real need in the community, but I couldn't do what I most wanted to. Jeanne stayed on the board and I was the one who left.

I continued looking for children's books and other teaching materials that included black people without stereotyping. I scoured bookstores, talked with teachers and librarians, and collected bibliographies. When I found the kinds of books I was looking for, I wrote to publishers and asked for donations. I identified myself as a member of the Upper Merion Fair Housing Council, told them why I was making the request, and promised to show the books to teachers. I received books from almost every publisher I contacted. When I found appropriate filmstrips and pictures, I paid for them myself.

In a few months I approached my local school district, Upper Merion, to see if I could set up an exhibit of my materials and talk to teachers at faculty meetings. The timing was in my favor because Pennsylvania was under state mandate to teach what they called "minority studies," and black students were beginning to come into the Upper Merion schools. After several meetings with administrators, I was invited to make presentations at faculty meetings in every school in the Upper Merion district: seven elementary schools, one junior high school, and one senior high school.

The week before the first faculty meeting, I took part in a demonstration at City Hall in Philadelphia. There had been ongoing violence against several black families who had moved to Kensington, one of the city's white residential districts. The mayor had not provided protection for them, and blamed the trouble on "outside agitators." Wanting some positive action to protect the black families, we held a peaceful vigil in front of the mayor's office. When we did not leave by the 4:00 deadline given us, we were arrested.

Unknown to me, my picture was taken as I was getting into the police van. That was on Friday. On Saturday, the picture appeared in the evening newspaper, the Philadelphia Bulletin. On Monday morning I received a call from the superintendent of the Upper Merion schools to inform me that all of my speaking engagements had been cancelled. I learned later that a member of the Upper Merion school board had been furious when she saw my picture in the paper. She telephoned the president of the board and he called an emergency meeting where it was agreed that I was a troublemaker. A memo was sent to every principal in the district, stating that Mrs. Baxter was never to be allowed in the schools as a speaker.

Eight-year-old Lisa and five-year-old Christie were proud of me, and I received many supportive calls from friends. Bruce admired my involvement with the fair housing council, but getting arrested and having it announced in the newspaper was a bit too much. He didn't speak to me for three days. Then he said mournfully, "Our life no longer revolves around me." He was right. The incident dramatized a change in our family; more and more, he had to fit his life around my plans and my schedule.

That same year, 1967, I began receiving invitations to speak at colleges, libraries, and schools in the Philadelphia area, usually as part of an in-service program to talk about Black history. With the state mandate and black parents and students demanding that Black history be added to the curricula, even predominantly white schools felt pressured to respond. Everywhere I went, I said that Black history is not only for black people, that white people need it just as much; it is all part of the American story.

During 1968 and 1969 I had many speaking engagements in white suburban schools, except Upper Merion where I had been banned. I usually took my exhibit with me, the collection I had made of books and other items. I spoke to teachers about the need for a more realistic view of American history, the white bias in most current teaching materials, and where to find things with a different perspective.

Along with many others who were going into schools during those years, I provided information about black people who had been left out of the history books. I thought many of the speakers put too much emphasis on who invented what, how many blacks fought in which war, who was the first black person to write a book or make a million dollars. I thought this approach cast black people into a heroic mold that made them not fully human. More importantly, it did not help white students understand why black people had acted as they had or against what odds.

I often told the story of Matthew Henson, a black explorer who accompanied Admiral Peary on all of his attempts to reach the North Pole. Henson was the only black member of the crew and the only one who got along well with the Eskimos. He made friends with them, learned their language, and became a skilled dog team driver. In the admiral's own words, Henson was his most valuable crew member. He was the one Peary chose to accompany him on the final dash to the Pole. It's a good story, full of suspense and drama that people always enjoyed.

But the rest of the story becomes uncomfortable. When Peary came back from the Pole, he and his crew members were honored. Everyone received a gold medal, even the cook and the cabin boy. Everyone, that is, except Matthew Henson. Years later, when Henson was an old man, President Eisenhower presented him with a silver medal for his part in reaching the Pole. As compensation for having been ignored so many years, Henson was offered a government job. The job he was offered? To be an office boy.

That was the part of the story that most people left out. I thought it was essential to tell because it would help students understand the depth of white resistance to racial justice and the roots of black anger. I urged teachers to use such stories as tools for re-evaluating not only the black role in U.S. history, but the white role as well. But most white teachers wanted nothing to do with it. Nor did they like to hear other stories I told. About our founding fathers extolling the virtues of freedom while owning slaves. About the Supreme Court ruling in favor of slave masters. About Andrew Jackson defying the U.S. Constitution when he expelled the Cherokee people from Georgia and sent them on the "Trail of Tears." White teachers thought I was stirring up trouble, that I was showing white people in a bad light and dragging our heroes in the dirt. "Let those things alone," they said, "let sleeping dogs lie."

There was always a split along color lines. After my presentation, black teachers were enthusiastic and smiling; they asked questions and shared stories. When I walked through the halls at the end of the program, white teachers often looked the other way.

A few white teachers lifted my spirits by telling me that I helped them make new and exciting discoveries. "You made me think about things I had never thought of before," said one man. Others told me that things I said would influence their teaching. But they were the exceptions. Many times I drove home in tears, drained from the emotional energy I put into my work and pained by the knowledge that many white teachers would not even speak to me.

Eventually I began to question what I was doing. Teachers went to in-service programs because they were required to, not because it was their choice. Suddenly, without preparation, some of their lifelong beliefs were being challenged. The programs didn't provide the time or structure for in-depth questions or meaningful give and take. There was usually no follow-up after I left, no support, no help in evaluating what they had heard.

I wondered if I was doing more harm than good. I wanted to share my stories in order to open doors, but maybe because of the feelings that were aroused, I was causing doors to be closed more tightly than ever. By the end of 1970, I decided that I would not do any more one-day workshops or be part of a program for people who did not choose to be there.

My work in the schools was just about over anyway. By 1971, the money for Black history was drying up, and I was no longer getting invitations. I wanted to find a way to reach white people without creating hostility, but schools were turning their attention to other things. There was nothing left for me to do but pack up my stories and go home.

Another Chance

I was thinking about applying for a teaching position in the Philadelphia public schools when I received a call from a teacher at Greene Street Friends School in the northwestern part of the city. She told me that all of the teachers there were white and the student body was about half and half, white and black. A number of teachers were having difficulty communicating with black parents, particularly in discussing anything to do with race. They wanted help. Would I come and talk with them?

At this Quaker elementary school, I met with five teachers and the principal, all women. Wanting to develop more understanding about race issues, they had decided to have a seminar that would meet once a week after school for the entire spring term. They asked me if I would design the seminar and be the coordinator.

I said I would do it if they agreed to two conditions. First, that they hire a black woman to work in partnership with me, for I believed the seminar would be more effective if coordinated by a black-white team. Second, that people participate in the seminar only if they chose to do so. The teachers readily agreed to both. I was delighted. This was just the chance I wanted.

For my partner, I chose a woman I had worked with in the fair housing council. In our first session at Greene Street Friends School, Frances and I helped the teachers clarify their goals. "What is it you want to work on during our time together?" we asked. They came up with a list of 15 questions and a name for the seminar: Racism in Education.

Frances and I prepared an agenda for each weekly meeting, in case the teachers didn't come up with something themselves. But they always did. Usually they wanted to share stories about things that happened in their classrooms. Once, the second grade teacher had shown her students a photograph of Martin Luther King being beaten by a policeman. The black children in her class were more upset by the picture than the white children, and later in the day a black child pummeled a white child. "Was that an act of retaliation?" the teacher asked. "Should I show the children pictures of violence?"

Another teacher described an incident which had occurred on a nature hike. While the children were looking at a beetle, the teacher commented that it was beautiful in spite of being black. She felt terrible because her comment indicated low esteem for blackness. Had she hurt the feelings of the black children who were present, or was she being overly sensitive to a small incident?

We sat quietly around the table while Evelyn told this story, clearly pained by what she had said. When someone suggested that perhaps she was harboring negative feelings about blackness, there was a tense moment of silence. Then Evelyn said yes, she thought it was true. That was a turning point in the seminar. From then on, everyone spoke more freely. They began sharing the stereotypes and prejudices they had previously been too ashamed to reveal.

Many times, the teachers got no clear answers to questions they brought to our gatherings. But that was less important than being able to talk about them. They learned to trust one another and to open themselves up. That seemed to me like the most important kind of learning. At the end of the spring term of 1971, the group decided to continue the seminar in the fall. Frances left in order to take a full-time job and Jane, another strong dynamic black woman, was hired as my co-coordinator.

The seminar at Greene Street Friends School marked a major shift in the way I worked. I encouraged participants to take the lead and direct the discussions. Instead of a lecturer, I became a facilitator, a role I found more satisfying.

When the seminar ended, I was hired as a part-time consultant to be on call for any member of the faculty who wanted to use my services. I did everything from finding photographs of Martin Luther King to helping design new programs as I worked with several teachers who wanted to add women, Native Americans and African Americans to their curricula. A big part of my job was digging for information and materials that teachers needed. I loved it.

If I continued this work, I needed to get some direct classroom experience in using the materials that I was recommending. The fourth grade teacher was leaving, so the following year I took her place. It had been twelve years since I had been a classroom teacher, concerned about the lily-white history book I was using. I looked forward to finally being able to use other kinds of materials.

Not long into the first semester, I realized that the materials were secondary. My interaction with the children was more important. I needed to help them recognize their biases. To make it safe for them to express their opinions. To guide them in listening respectfully to others in the group. To help them examine critically the things they saw and heard and read. This was the real challenge, the real excitement.

Before I began a unit of study on Lenape Indians -- Native American people who had lived in the Philadelphia area -- I asked the children what came to mind when they heard the word "Indian." They said tomahawk, scalping, war paint, moccasins, etc. I wrote each word on a separate piece of paper and put it on a bulletin board. For weeks, those words were there. Most were stereotypes, many of them associated with violence.

During that time, we read books about Lenape Indians, corresponded with a Lenape woman, borrowed photographs and artifacts from a museum, as well as replicas of Lenape houses, to keep in our classroom for a month. We wrote plays and stories and did dramatizations. By the time we finished the unit, the children no longer liked the words that were on the bulletin board. We replaced them with information about the Lenape people. The children then began spotting stereotypes of Native Americans in story books and became angry with authors who didn't know any better.

The children also wanted to know more about African Americans. They loved the biographies I read to them, and began asking for others in the library. When the whole school went to the auditorium to watch a film on Martin Luther King, my children came back to the classroom and discussed it heatedly.

One day I showed them a film about Harriet Tubman, portraying her as a slave in Maryland, then planning her escape. The children were spellbound. When Tubman finally crossed the border into Pennsylvania and knew she was free, the children cheered. Raised fists went into the air. Black fists and white fists. Those children were back a hundred years in time, hiding in a wagon that carried them to freedom.

Then came an event that at first seemed unrelated. Every time they had the chance, the boys were in the school yard playing soccer. Sweaty, grimy boys yelling and laughing. And there was Nada. Every day, while the boys were playing, Nada in her clean dress was sitting on the stone wall next to the field. Sitting and watching the soccer game with longing in her eyes. Finally I asked her if she wanted to play. "Only boys play soccer," she said.

"But if you could, would you want to play?"

"Yes," she said, "but they'd never let me."

I said, "Nada, there's no reason why only boys should play soccer. What if I help you?"

It was then that Nada turned to look at me. "Would you?" she asked, her face coming to life. We walked back into the building arm in arm, like conspirators. We were about to open a can of worms.

When I told the boys what Nada wanted, they were incensed. Who ever heard of girls playing soccer! They couldn't run worth a darn, they couldn't kick a ball, they'd cry if somebody knocked them down, they would fall all over the playing field and ruin the game. In their anger and frustration, the boys began slamming things and kicking the legs of their desks. Then they were despairing. They would never play soccer again. Life was over.

For the girls, it was the opposite. Suddenly a door had opened to new possibilities. For the first time, they thought it might be fun to play soccer, and they told Nada they would like to join her. That was the beginning of two weeks of intense struggle. I didn't want to simply announce that from then on girls would be allowed to play and the boys had to accept it, no questions asked. I wanted them to do whatever they needed in order to work it through. I hoped the class would arrive at consensus.

Nothing else that year was as emotion-laden as the issue of whether or not girls should play soccer. The girls put forth all their arguments for the affirmative, the boys held onto their reasons why it would be a total disaster. The boys were gloomy and ill-tempered, and the girls had new energy. Only the two or three boys who did not play soccer had any sympathy for the girls. Otherwise, it completely united the children. Race was not an issue, only gender. Black boys and white boys against black girls and white girls.

But it was race that finally broke the deadlock. One day I asked if they remembered what happened when the first black baseball players tried to break into the major leagues. Of course they remembered; we had talked about it in class. They had been indignant that black players had been treated so badly.

"Tell me the reasons the major leagues gave for not letting black players in," I said. "Stupid reasons," answered the boys. "They said the black players couldn't play as well and would ruin the game. Baseball would never be the same."

"Are those arguments any different from the ones you're using against the girls?" I asked. The boys squirmed and muttered, but could not come up with an answer. That day the class achieved consensus: anyone who wanted to play soccer could play.

In the afternoon, when the children came in from their first game together, all of them were beaming. The boys couldn't wait to tell me the news. Wow, they said, that Alison sure can run! And Nada made a goal, and the others could really use their feet, and...and... and....To the boys, a miracle had occurred: the game had not been ruined. For the girls, it was a different kind of miracle: something they had assumed was closed had opened.

Only Nada continued to play soccer for the rest of the year. One by one, the other girls dropped out and went back to their more usual activities. They had won their right to play, which was all they needed. Mission accomplished.

I was excited about what happened. Not only could girls now play soccer, the experience made teachers think about other ways in which we might be setting limits on girls without realizing it. I was happy about the validation I felt for my work. I had watched my students grow in awareness and concern about racial issues, and now they had connected these issues in a tangible way to their own lives.

I taught fourth grade for another year at Greene Street Friends School, but I was feeling confined by being in the classroom. I wanted to spend more time with teachers and try my hand at writing curriculum materials. Several principals of Quaker schools in the Philadelphia area contacted me about working with them and tried to get the Friends Council on Education to help with funding. When I spoke at Friends' conferences, I was received with enthusiasm. When I visited schools, principals and teachers were excited about my work. But nothing came of it; no one seemed to have the money to hire me.

I decided to try my hand at being a school librarian. Perhaps in that capacity, I would be able to work with both teachers and students, using my experience of the past four years. In September 1975 I enrolled in the master's program at the School of Library Science at Drexel University. Maybe this would give me another chance to do the things I wanted to do.

"I Want to Be Free"

In addition to my work at the library school, I wanted to write a social studies program for children in the middle grades. Not sure how to get started, I went to the Greene Street Friends School library to get some ideas. Nothing clicked until I found myself taking an unfamiliar book off of the shelf. It was *Mumbet: The Story of Elizabeth Freeman*, by Harold W. Felton. By the time I finished reading the story, I knew I had found what I wanted.

Elizabeth Freeman was a black slave called Betty or Bet, and later Mumbet. Mum probably meant mother. Mother Bet. Felton writes that around 1750, when Mumbet was six months old, she was purchased by John Ashley and taken to his home in southwestern Massachusetts. Ashley fought in the Revolutionary War. He was one of the framers of the Declaration of Rights in 1773, a document which has been called America's first Declaration of

Independence. John Ashley was a man who loved freedom and owned slaves.

In l780 a group of men gathered at Ashley's home to write a constitution for the new state of Massachusetts. Mumbet, who was probably about 30 by then, served the men food and ale as they wrote and later when they celebrated the completion of their work. She heard the words they had written: all men are born free and equal. She saw how happy they were, how proud of themselves for writing this into the constitution.

If these leaders believed so ardently in freedom, she thought, then freedom must be on the way. Her husband, who had been killed in the Revolutionary War, would not have died in vain. Her daughter, Little Bet, would grow up as a free person. But as time went on, it became clear that the freedom these white men had in mind did not include her.

One day, Mumbet heard Mrs. Ashley screaming at Lizzie, another slave in the Ashley home. Mumbet ran to the kitchen and found Lizzie crouching on the floor next to the fireplace, with her hands on her head. Mrs. Ashley was standing over her, holding a red-hot shovel in the air, about to swing it down. Mumbet rushed over to Lizzie and threw her arm out to ward off the blow. The shovel landed on Mumbet's arm, cutting it to the bone.

Mrs. Ashley and her husband were full of apologies for Mumbet's injury, and promised never to hurt her again. But the incident made Mumbet resolve that she would no longer be a slave. Shortly afterwards, she walked four miles to the village of Sheffield to find the office of Theodore Sedgwick. He was a lawyer and one of the men who met at John Ashley's house to write the Massachusetts constitution. Theodore Sedgwick was the only one of those men who had treated Mumbet with respect. Each day when he arrived, he looked her in the eye and said good morning. He thanked her when she served his ale. She hoped that he would now help her gain her freedom.

Mumbet told Sedgwick that since the state constitution said that all men are free and equal, then she should not be a slave. Sedgwick did not own slaves, but he was stunned by Mumbet's request to help her gain her freedom. Yet fairly soon he began the legal proceedings that took her to court. Mumbet won her freedom thanks to the words in the constitution that her slave master had helped to write.

As a free person, she lived with the Sedgwicks for several years, employed as a housekeeper. Eventually she purchased her own house. Working as a nurse, she supported herself and educated her grandchildren and great-grandchildren. She was buried in the Sedgwick family plot in the cemetery in Stockbridge, Massachusetts.

I loved Mumbet's quiet strength and courage, and I loved the teaching possibilities that lay within her story. It showed that slavery existed in the north as well as the south, it portrayed people who had different ways of looking at slavery, and it provided an opportunity to see that right and wrong are not always clearly separated. It's easy to hate slavery when the master is hard and vicious. You know who's good and who's bad. But John Ashley was not a vicious person. I wanted children to see a piece of history that is filled with struggles between our visions and our realities. The story of Mumbet was a vehicle for doing that.

Not much learning would take place, though, if children didn't like the book. Bea, the new fourth grade teacher at Greene Street Friends School, read it to her students, and told me they loved it. That's all I needed to know; I was ready to begin writing.

While continuing my studies at Drexel, I took a full-time job at an educational research center. I squeezed the writing I wanted to do into an hour here, two hours there, whatever time I could carve out for myself between home, school, and job. I later cut back on my job from five days a week to four. Fridays became my own, and I looked forward to them eagerly. I was either in my study at home with the phone turned off, or I was tucked away in the quiet of the library at Haverford or Bryn Mawr College.

One time I spent several days at a cabin we had in the Pocono Mountains. I loaded the car with typewriter, table, floor lamp, food, all my papers, and our dog. When I arrived, I turned off the phone and for four glorious days I wrote. When I was hungry, I popped prepared food into the oven. When I needed a break, I took the dog for a walk. On the walks, I thought through problems and clarified ideas. I worked until my eyes were bleary and I could do nothing except fall into bed. Those days were a precious gift. It was the only time my writing didn't fit around other people's schedules.

My plan was to write three lessons for the story of Mumbet, but I kept on going. By the time I finished, I had written 18 lessons. One of them focused on differing views of slavery. I wanted children to think about these points of view and why people thought the way they did. I wrote a lesson about profit, the meaning of the word, and in what ways slavery was profitable.

Other lessons included information about black soldiers in the Continental Army and about the Declaration of Independence. I wrote guidelines for role plays, a reference book that included a chronology of important events, biographies, and a glossary. I made a map of the colonies in 1775, several puzzles, and 18 detailed lesson plans. Mumbet was no longer the focus. Her story was now the introduction to a program about slavery at the time of the American Revolution. Her words became the title of the program: "I Want to Be Free."

In the fall of l977, with "I Want to Be Free" nearly complete, I was ready to begin testing. Bea, the fourth grade teacher at Greene Street Friends School, agreed to give the program its trial run. It was exciting to watch my creation unfold. The children raised their hands eagerly, worked in small groups, and talked animatedly. The role play was particularly exciting. Power went to the head of the boy who played the part of King George. The rest of the children were colonists who got really disgusted with the tyrannical king, went outside for recess and planned an insurrection. What a wonderful conversation they had when Bea sat them down for debriefing! She invited me to take part, but I just watched and listened. And I smiled. It was really working.

Field Testing

To do more testing of the program, I set my sights on Kensington where, a few years earlier, the violence against black families had set in motion a series of events that led to my being barred from speaking in the Upper Merion schools. Kensington was a white working class neighborhood with a reputation for being the most racist part of Philadelphia. I figured that if "I Want to Be Free" worked there, it could work anywhere. I made an appointment with the Assistant Superintendent in charge of curriculum in the Philadelphia schools. Within two weeks he met with me, read "I Want to Be Free," and gave me permission for field testing.

I pointed out that my program was not Black history. "It's history that everyone needs," I explained, "it's supplementary to the existing textbooks, and just as important for white children as for black." The Assistant Superintendent nodded in agreement. Then he picked up the phone, called the Director of African American Studies and said he was turning me and my program over to his department. So much for the pitch that it wasn't Black history, but I decided not to press my point.

I asked to have the program taught in a number of schools in different parts of the city so I could compare results. The Director of African American Studies thought it was a good idea and promised to find the schools for me to work with, but he was skeptical about Kensington. "Do you know what you'll be getting into?" he asked. "Those folks don't want anything to do with black." Nevertheless, he was game for me to give it a try, and he had a teacher in mind. If anyone could pull it off, it would be Laree (la REE) Owens, a woman of boundless energy and enthusiasm. He made an appointment for me to meet her.

A week later I went to Kensington and found Sheridan School, a typical old-style school, gray stone, massive and solid. A stern, no-nonsense building. I introduced myself to the principal, then climbed the stairs to the third floor and knocked on the door of a fifth/sixth grade classroom. Laree Owens greeted me warmly. While her children were busy with an assignment, she and I talked about "I Want to Be Free." Laree's eyes sparkled as I described the program. She began spinning out ideas about teaching it and about the variations she might want to make.

Laree was the teacher I'd been hoping for, enthusiastic about the program and willing to teach it in spite of the controversy it might provoke. Laree said I was just the person she had been hoping would come along, that my program was exactly the kind of thing she had been looking for. But she hesitated. Eight years earlier, when she was one of the first black teachers assigned to Sheridan, angry white parents had patrolled the hall outside her classroom. Things were thrown at her on the street and tires were stolen from her car. By the time I met her, she had won the respect of the children and their parents. She didn't want them to turn against her again.

Four months later, Laree agreed to work with me, but she made two stipulations. First, that we work together as a team and that I come frequently to her classroom. She wanted support in case she was criticized for teaching this material. As a white person, I would give the project credibility in the eyes of the community. Second, she said, "We must call the program American history. It will not survive a day if we call it Black history." I had no trouble accepting her terms. In the spring of 1978, I tested "I Want to Be Free" in six Philadelphia schools. Two were racially mixed, two were all black, and two were all white. I had good teachers and responsive children and I loved working in all six schools, but my heart was in Kensington. That's where the program would be put to the greatest test.

Laree's students were a special class. All of them had difficulties, both socially and academically; they were labeled the dummies and troublemakers of the school. Laree was determined that these children would succeed in her class and begin to feel good about themselves. She thought she would rewrite parts of "I Want to Be Free" to make the reading easier but found that she didn't have to. When I visited at the end of the first lesson, Laree was glowing. She told me the children loved the program and were reading it without much trouble. For the first time, they were enjoying social studies.

The children were happy to see me, eager to tell me about Mumbet and how much they liked her. Laree asked some questions to get them started, but they didn't need much prodding. These white children were excited to be learning about black people. One day a girl came up to me after class and shyly said, "Mrs. Baxter, I like your program a lot." When I asked her why, she said she never knew before that black people were important.

Another day, a girl said that she had been in the supermarket and was upset when she saw a white woman being rude to a black woman. As we talked about it, the children realized that such incidents were common but they had never noticed them before. The children were beginning to be aware of the difficulties for black people in their community.

At Laree's request, I gave her extra copies of *Mumbet: The Story of Elizabeth Freeman* for children to take home to show their parents. One girl told me her mother loved the book and wondered why she never learned about Mumbet when she was in school. Another girl read the book to her grandmother who had cancer. "When I read the story to my grandmother," the girl said, "she she loved the story so much that didn't feel her pain."

One day the students asked why the "I Want to Be Free" program spent so much time on black people. To answer that question, I decided to do a role-play. I took the children to the auditorium and seated them in different areas, dividing them into three groups: black slaves, rich white folks, and poor white folks. I asked who owned most of the land. The rich white folks raised their hands. Who owned most of the businesses? Again, the rich white folks raised their hands. With each question, the children answered without hesitation. They understood how these groups related to each other and who had the power. It didn't take them long to decide who wrote the newspapers and the books, and who decided how history was written. Then it was easy for them to answer their own question about "I Want to Be Free." They saw that black people had been left out of history. After that, the children began going to the school library for biographies of black people. Not finding many there, they looked in the public library and asked the school librarian to purchase the books they wanted.

One day I told them about black people in other periods of history. They loved the stories of Robert Smalls, Rosa Parks, Mary McLeod Bethune, Malcolm X, and Fannie Lou Hamer. They were sad at their hardships and cheered their triumphs. In the middle of my storytelling, Laree left the room. A few minutes later, she returned with the principal. When he walked in, he saw thirty spell-bound children, and the only sound in the room was my voice. Laree wanted the principal to see what was happening in this class of children who had the reputation of being such troublemakers that they would never sit still for anything.

One of the boys in Laree's class always used the word nigger, and I couldn't understand why she never corrected him. Then one day, during a class discussion, he said something about black people. After class, Laree told me that the boy had made the change himself, without any pressure. "It's your program that did it," she said, "the child just got to the point where his feelings changed enough for him to no longer want to use that word." But I give most of the credit to Laree. She was wise enough to care not so much about changing the child's behavior but about providing the atmosphere where he could change it himself. It's one of my most treasured memories of her.

In June, Laree wanted her class to visit the African American Museum in Philadelphia. She made arrangements for it to be a joint trip with the children from Greene Street Friends School who had first used the "I Want to Be Free" program. This was the first time Sheridan students had ever been with a racially mixed group.

After a tour of the museum, we had lunch in a nearby park. As the children played together, the five adults sat on benches and watched them: Laree, two white mothers of Sheridan students, a black woman from the school administration, and me. We talked about how beautiful it was to see the children completely at ease with one another. This was a new experience for the two Sheridan mothers and they were having as good a time as everyone else.

The children were sad when the program was over. I was too, for I would miss them. And I would miss Laree who had brought my program to life in this community where I wanted so much for it to succeed. The experience surpassed all my expectations. The children had opened their hearts and their minds more than I could have imagined. Over the summer I made a few revisions to the program, then considered it a finished product.

My daughters were young women by then. Lisa was in Kenya that summer, spending a year as a student at Friends World College. This Quaker school, based on Long Island, required students to study in two different countries as part of their academic program. The following year, Lisa would go to Jerusalem and Christie would join her so they could travel together at the end of the semester.

Return to Sheridan

The girls were still away when Laree called in the spring of 1979. We hadn't talked with each other since we finished testing "I Want to Be Free" the previous year. She was excited about something that was going on at Sheridan School and wanted me to visit.

All along, Laree had seen the potential for desegregation growing out of the "I Want to Be Free" program. Now she told me that her dream was coming true. "I talked to my students after we went to the museum last year," she said.

"Everybody had such a good time on that trip, including the parents, and I never heard a word of complaint from anybody about being with black children." So Laree asked her students how they would feel about going to school with black children. They said they didn't see why not; they wondered why she was making a point of it. Laree asked if they felt that way before "I Want to Be Free." Then the children realized that before the program, they would have said no.

Laree got a positive response from teachers as well as students. That fall, the principal, some faculty members, and a group of parents designed a desegregation plan. From the district superintendent's office came the word that such a plan would never work in Kensington; it was risking too much white hostility. The group at Sheridan went ahead without the support of the district office. The first part of the plan was an exchange program with an all-black school in another part of Philadelphia. For two weeks in the spring of 1980, 30 white fifth and sixth graders from Sheridan would attend classes at the Ada Lewis Middle School, and 30 black students from Ada Lewis would come to Sheridan. Again the response came from the administration: "It can't be done. Not in this neighborhood."

But it *was* done. And it was a great success. That was when Laree called and asked me to spend a day at Sheridan. She wanted me to go to each of the four classes in the exchange program, tell the story of Mumbet, and take photographs. The day I was there, I met the district superintendent in the hall. He told me that when he heard the exchange program was going well, he had to see for himself. He had never imagined that what was taking place would be possible. He was thrilled to see black children and white children attending classes, eating lunch, and playing together as though it was the most natural thing in the world. Nobody had burned a cross in front of the school. No one had so much as called and registered a complaint.

I went back on the last day of the exchange, and watched as the children said goodbye to one another. There on the streets of Kensington, black children and white children hugged one another and cried because they wouldn't see each other again. Through the windows of the buses, black hands reached out and linked with white hands until the buses began to move away.

Shortly after that, the district superintendent invited me to a meeting at his office to hear his principals talk about the exchange program. They were excited about it and hoped it had set a precedent. They wanted to discuss which schools might work in pairs for other exchange programs. The district superintendent introduced me to the principals, but my name was not mentioned again. No one looked at me or asked me to make any comments or even suggested that I had anything to do with what happened at Sheridan. Not a word was said about "I Want to Be Free." Nevertheless, I left the meeting feeling hopeful. If these principals are so excited about the exchange program, I thought, and want to try it elsewhere, then surely they will be interested in me. After all, it was "I Want to Be Free" that started the whole thing. I hoped the school district would purchase my materials and hire me as an independent consultant.

Meanwhile, Sheridan School was working on the next step of its desegregation plan: recruitment of full-time black students. That fall, when black students began attending the school, they were bused in and welcomed without trouble. Sheridan was the first public school in Philadelphia to desegregate on a completely voluntary basis.

The following spring, Laree and three other teachers decided to teach "I Want to Be Free" to all fifth and sixth grade students at the school. The teachers wanted to work together as a team and asked me to join them, along with the librarian and the art teacher. Two of the teachers were black, the rest of us white. All of the classes included black students. The school paid me for the materials, but I gave my time free of charge.

Laree wanted me to teach the first lesson of "I Want to Be Free" to all four classes together in the auditorium. The teachers would teach lesson two the following week in their own classrooms. The week after that I would do lesson three in the auditorium. And so on. I thought it was a crazy idea. How could I teach a lesson to over a hundred children at the same time? I said I'd have to think about it, but it was hard to say no to Laree. I agreed to do it on one condition: that the teachers involved would always be present at those large-group gatherings. I wanted their active participation. And to my amazement, her plan worked. I learned how to keep the children's interest with stories, role plays, games, and dramatic ways of presenting the lesson. We had a good time.

Laree had some real wisdom behind her plan. Desegregation was working well in the school, but the teachers were still concerned about community response. They felt more secure working together as a team on a program that might cause some hostility. Their enthusiasm was contagious. Other teachers asked about what was going on, and wanted to know if they could sit in on some of our classes.

Once more, I was seeing my creation come to life, but this time I was an active participant and had a privileged position in the school. Everyone was happy to see me and treated me as though I was special. I had kind of a grandmother role with the children. I was a treat for them, breaking up the routine of the day; then I could walk out and leave the teachers with the real responsibility.

Chuck Stone was a popular local black newspaper columnist. When he heard what was happening at Sheridan, he asked if he could visit. He went to all four classrooms where "I Want to Be Free" was being taught, observed lessons and talked with students and teachers. It was an exciting day at Sheridan! It was good timing because the teachers' fears about community criticism seemed to be coming true. A number of parents had raised questions about "I Want to Be Free." They didn't like all that emphasis on black people, and they thought it was taking time away from the basics. These parents were talking about mobilizing others to get "I Want to Be Free" out of the school.

Then came Chuck's visit and his newspaper column in which he praised the school warmly. He said that at Sheridan School "American education is enjoying one of its proudest moments as all of the elements necessary for success come together and work -- concerned parents, a dedicated principal, skilled teachers, enthusiastic students, an interesting curriculum, a commitment to quality education and the implementation of racial integration." The column was posted prominently in the school hall. Teachers and students and parents were radiant. Nothing further was said about getting rid of "I Want to Be Free."

In June that year, 1980, the four classes put on a show for the entire school and another performance for parents. With the American Revolution as the theme, it was a big undertaking that took weeks of planning. My role was to help a number of children write and produce a play that was to be part of the program. Deciding to dramatize Elizabeth Freeman winning her freedom, the children threw themselves into the job with great energy. They worked day after day to get the script just right.

We had already done a lot of role playing. Everyone wanted to be Mumbet, and all of them had taken her part --

black or white, boy or girl, it didn't matter. Whichever child played Mumbet seemed to grow to fill the role. Even the shyest girl began to talk in a strong voice and stand tall as she faced her master and told him she had a right to be free.

When the program was finally ready, the children performed in the morning for the rest of the school. Students filled every available seat in the auditorium and had to bring extra chairs. That afternoon, at the performance for parents, there was standing room only. The auditorium was packed with mothers, fathers, and grandparents. People in stay-at-home clothes, work clothes and police uniforms. To everyone's excitement, the crew from a local television channel showed up to film the show for a two-minute spot on the evening news. If I could have chosen those two minutes, I would have picked the part of the play where Mumbet demanded her freedom. And that's exactly what I saw on TV that evening.

The play was the most popular part of the program. When a white girl, playing the part of a slave, stood up to her master and demanded her freedom, there was not a sound in the auditorium. I looked around and saw rapt faces. When Mumbet won her freedom in the courtroom, the audience broke out into cheers and applause. At the end of the program, Laree and I were called up to the stage and presented with flowers.

The audience left, the children went back to their lessons, and my time at Sheridan was over. I went to the four classrooms to say my goodbyes, where I got hugs and kisses and words of appreciation. One of the white teachers said to me, with tears in his eyes, that they all loved me, that I had made a difference to the school, and I would be missed.

And oh, how I loved the school! It had made a difference to me, as well. It helped me know that people can find their way past fear and hatred and violence. I learned that when I did the testing at Sheridan two years earlier. I knew it more than ever when I stood on the stage that afternoon, holding my flowers and looking out into the faces of those working class people, mostly white, who were beaming at me and applauding. My eyes filled with tears as I stood there. Those might just as well have been my grandparents, my friends, my neighbors, my colleagues. For by then it seemed that within all of us, there is the capacity for change.

One Way or Another

I turned fifty in March of 1980, three months before my goodbyes at Sheridan. I was thrilled by my experiences there, but miserably unhappy in my marriage. Hanging in with the marriage hadn't helped, and neither had therapy. By the end of the school year, I was ready to begin the process of separation.

Earlier that year, Lisa and I had gone to an orientation weekend of Movement for a New Society (MNS). MNS was a network of people who believed in changing society through nonviolent means. Started by radical Quakers, it attracted people from the civil rights and anti-war movements, feminism and the counterculture. It was centered in West Philadelphia, a neighborhood with a mix of people: black, white, Asian, working class and professional, as well as people living in poverty. MNS members lived communally in large old houses where they shared chores and expenses.

I was attracted not only to MNS, but to a man I met at the orientation weekend. George Fischer lived in Woodstock, New York. He had grown up in the Soviet Union and come to this country when he was 16, speaking German and Russian, and one sentence of English in order to say that he was very happy to be in America. He earned a Ph.D. at Harvard and taught at Ivy League schools, but disliked their elitism and was now happily teaching at City University of New York. Barely into our first conversation, I fell in love with George. Over the next five years, he would become an increasingly important part of my life.

Toward the end of summer, I rented an old Victorian seven-bedroom house in the same neighborhood as most of the MNS activities. It was large enough for Christie, Lisa, and me, two university students and a young married couple we recruited in order to share the expenses.

When my divorce from Bruce was finalized, I had no guaranteed income. For the next few years I would have to figure out how to support Lisa, Christie, and myself. It was a big help when Bruce and I sold our house in King of Prussia and split the profits. When the money ran out, my long-time and dearest friends, Marge, Ethel, and Julie, loaned me some money. Lisa, who was 22, got a full-time job and made a commitment to support us for a year. I accepted her offer with gratitude mixed with guilt. I should have been the one to get a full-time job, but I never did; I kept hoping that I would begin to earn money from the work I loved.

One of the things I learned that year was how to avoid making payments on time. Sometimes I "forgot" to sign my check, which never earned me a penalty, but gave me another week or so while the check was returned for my signature. Often I paid only part of my bill at a time. The gas company let me work out a payment plan when $400.00 was overdue; it took months for me to pay it off. Another way I managed was by not buying clothes. For going to schools, I wore two good outfits left over from my King of Prussia days. The brown was for fall and winter, the navy blue for spring.

I became a member of MNS, but my highest priority was working to promote "I Want to Be Free." I began by submitting the program to the Philadelphia School District for evaluation. A couple of months later, the program was placed on the school district's approved list of teaching materials, which meant that I could begin making sales.

I had just received a call from the Associate Superintendent who was in charge of desegregation for the School District of Philadelphia. He had heard about the Sheridan experience and wanted to meet with me to see how my work might be promoted in other schools. This was a man of influence in the school district. I had heard high praise for him from numerous people, and was delighted that he had contacted me. The Associate Superintendent was a tall, distinguished looking white man. He was thoughtful and clear, did not engage in superficial courtesy. With little explanation on my part, he understood my goals and what excited me. He told me that he wanted to promote my work in the school district, but the money didn't exist; he would have to find it. I knew that money was a problem, but the meeting buoyed my spirits. With this door at such a high level now open to me, surely other doors would follow.

When a part-time job came along, I jumped at the opportunity. The Crossing was an MNS house where meetings, trainings, and social gatherings were held. The house needed renovations, and MNS members decided to do the work themselves under the guidance of an older member who was an experienced builder. Any of us who worked on the house would get paid $5.00 an hour. Figuring this would keep us in groceries for a few months, I joined the crew.

I knew nothing about building, but I wasn't the only one. My first day on the job, I was sent to the basement, along with another novice, where we learned how to mix cement and throw it on the wall. Later, a professional carpenter taught me how to put up dry wall and tape it.

Each day I left the job exhausted and covered with white dust, but I had a great sense of satisfaction. I never knew what would happen in schools, but here I could see immediately what I had accomplished: the old wall I had plastered or the new wall I had built, or the cabinets I had put up.

I took a Dale Carnegie sales course, a completely new experience for me. In a class composed mostly of salespeople, I was a misfit. The agent who signed me up told me later he thought I'd never make it through the program. He was right in thinking that sales was not exactly my calling, but the course taught me how to organize my time and plan my approach to schools.

Every week I spent many hours on the phone, trying to contact principals of elementary and middle schools. It could take as many as six calls to find one available. Then I introduced myself, described "I Want to Be Free," and asked if I could talk to the teachers. Out of twenty completed calls, I'd get eight to ten appointments to make a presentation at a faculty meeting. I needed to talk directly to teachers; if they weren't interested, I didn't stand a chance of making a sale.

While I was approaching schools one by one, I was also trying to get access to administrators at the central office. The school district was in a bind. On the one hand they were under heavy federal pressure to desegregate. On the other hand they had fierce resistance in a number of white communities where angry parents demonstrated in the streets, determined not to have their schools integrated. The work that Laree and I did at Sheridan had calmed white fears and been a catalyst for quiet successful desegregation. I thought if people in the central administration only knew about it, they would give us the chance to try the program elsewhere. Laree said she would leave Sheridan and work with me anywhere in the city.

I knocked on doors, wrote letters, and talked to anybody who might put in a good word for me. While continuing to teach at Sheridan, Laree made her own attempts to reach people who had the power to make decisions. But their doors were closed and their secretaries well trained to keep them that way. In 1982, after two years of our efforts, we hadn't made a dent.

I still hoped that the Associate Superintendent, who had expressed an interest in promoting my work, would be able to help me. He was a candidate for superintendent and if he was selected, I might be in an even better position. But in the fall of 1982, it was Constance Clayton who was chosen, becoming Philadelphia's first black woman superintendent of schools. She gave the associate superintendent a less influential job, and he no longer had a role in desegregation. I never heard from him again.

By then, I was taking "I Want to Be Free" into the suburbs. It was hard to make contacts because administrators in these predominantly white school districts did not see the need for materials that dealt with black people. I was not allowed to speak at faculty meetings; I had to leave sample materials at the school and let the principal or social studies coordinator show them to teachers. That left me with my hands tied, for no one else could present the program the way I could.

Over and over, I had the same experience. Administrators told me they admired my work and my dedication. They said my program was well written and interesting, and that it might be very valuable. Then a couple of weeks later I would get a phone call asking me to pick up my materials. There would be a polite but brief message that "I Want to Be Free" did not fit their curriculum needs.

It was much the same when I made presentations at administrators' meetings in different parts of the state. Sometimes people told me that my talk had made the whole day worthwhile. Many of them expressed admiration for the work I was doing and the message I was carrying to the schools. One woman said, "Why, you're a missionary!" I think she meant it as a compliment, but people don't usually invite missionaries to come home with them. They wished me well, but did not buy my materials or my services.

In the spring of 1983, I seemed to be getting a lucky break. The social studies coordinator for a suburban school district expressed an interest in "I Want to Be Free" and asked me to leave seven classroom sets with her, one for each of the principals of the elementary schools in the district. A couple of weeks later she called to tell me the principals loved the program and wanted to purchase it for the following school term. Their plan was to make it the core curriculum for social studies in all seven schools. Asians were moving into this district which had long been predominantly white, and tensions were beginning to surface. The principals of the elementary schools believed that "I Want to Be Free" would help reduce those tensions.

I had one more meeting with the social studies coordinator and we set a date for me to meet the principals. She said they wanted to start making plans for me to play a role in their history program beginning that September. It was more than I had imagined possible, and I was very excited.

Then came the phone call asking me to pick up my materials. This time it was the school board that stood in the way. Two things were up for consideration: the "I Want to Be Free" project, and setting up a computer program. Since there was not enough money for both, the members of the board had to make a choice. They voted for computers.

It was one of my lowest points. Soon after that, I was on West River Drive in Philadelphia with some time between school appointments. I parked the car and sat on a bench next to the Schuylkill River. I held a copy of the Teacher's Guide to "I Want to Be Free," intending to check something before I went to the next school. As I looked at the river, I had an urge to toss the book into the water and watch it sink out of sight. It would be so easy. All I had to do was put "I Want to Be Free" into a watery grave and I would be released from having to go through one more disappointment. I felt old and tired.

If teachers hadn't liked my program, I would have decided that it wasn't good enough. But over and over, they expressed their enthusiasm. Often at faculty meetings I watched teachers file in at the end of their teaching day, wanting to be anywhere but at a meeting, and then brighten up when I talked to them. Some of them told me afterwards that it was the best faculty meeting they'd ever had. I felt their longing to break through the rigidity of the school system, to be able to choose programs outside the constraints of the curriculum that was set for them. It didn't have to be "I Want to Be Free." It could have been some other program, but I held a promise of things they wanted.

I made a trickle of sales, but was stymied at the higher administrative levels. Principals could not purchase directly from me; they had to submit their orders to the central administration. Eventually I would receive an official order from the proper department downtown. Only then could I deliver the goods, submit my bill, and know I would be paid. Somewhere in the administrative labyrinth, more than half of my orders disappeared. Many frustrated principals told me they had teachers looking forward to using "I Want to Be Free," but there was nothing they could do if their order did not go through. It was a common experience, they said. No matter what they were ordering, they never knew if they would receive it.

That's what made me so discouraged the day I sat by the river. It was the administration, always the administration. I didn't know how to get past their endless stonewalling. But I couldn't stop thinking about the teachers. They were the ones who made me feel that I had to keep trying. I picked up my Teacher's Guide, went back to the car, and drove to my next appointment.

A couple of months later, I decided to approach the Catholic school system in Philadelphia. I had no contacts there, but it was easy to get an appointment at the central administration with the Sister in charge of curriculum. A pleasant woman, she was happy to tell me who to see next, but she gave me little hope. She said, "If this were ten years ago when we had riot squads in our schools because of racial tension, I would put your program in every school in our system. But there is no urgency now." I felt discouraged and angry. It was the same story everywhere. People looked for remedies when things blew up, but who was doing the healing that might keep the violence from happening?

Nevertheless, I contacted the woman the Sister had suggested. She was an elementary school principal and chair of the social studies committee. I couldn't talk to anyone else without her approval. I finally reached her on the phone, only to be greeted with a stern: "And who are *you*?" But she made an appointment with me, and in person she was exceedingly cordial. She took me to meet teachers and visit classes in her school, and invited me to submit "I Want to Be Free" to the social studies committee. If the program met with the committee's approval, then it would be placed on the approved list of the Archdiocese schools. Only then would I be allowed to visit individual schools to make sales.

I was referred to another Sister, also the principal of an elementary school. I was told she was the most influential member of the social studies committee; if "I Want to Be Free" got her endorsement, the program would be approved. I spent a day at her school, gave her sample materials, visited classes, told stories, and taught a demonstration lesson. That afternoon she said she would recommend the program.

A couple of weeks later, the chair of the social studies committee informed me that "I Want to Be Free" had been passed by the committee, and would be placed on the list of approved materials for the Archdiocese schools. All I had to do was receive official word to that effect from the central administration and learn the procedures for visiting schools. But it never happened. In the spring and summer of 1984 I made numerous phone calls, but could not get past a secretary. The two principals I had met did not come to the phone, return my calls or answer my letters. For a time, in disbelief that they would drop me without explanation, I continued to make calls. But there was no point to it. The first Sister I had met was right. There were no riot squads on duty, and the Catholic schools were not going to buy my program.

I had no better luck in the suburbs. There was only one district left where I had any hope of succeeding. The social studies coordinator tried to promote "I Want to Be Free," but he could not get past the roadblocks any more than I could. I picked up my materials and closed my files on the suburban schools.

I was exhausted and not making enough money even to cover expenses. Knowing I could no longer go on by myself, I teamed up with two friends in MNS who shared my concerns about race and diversity. Linda came from India and had lived many years in Tanzania. David was Chinese-American. The three of us incorporated and called ourselves The Multicultural Resource Center. We hoped to eventually have a center where teachers could come to see materials and attend workshops and seminars. Linda began writing proposals. David and I began writing an Asian-American program.

With renewed energy, I plunged into these projects. David and I also took part-time jobs with the Nationalities

Service Center, going into elementary and junior high school classes to present Green Circle, a program promoting the acceptance of differences.

Holding On

I was sick during the winter of 1984, a flu-like illness that started before the holidays and lasted nearly four weeks. In the middle of January, I decided I was ready to go back to work. Believing I was well again, I was happy to ride the trolley into town and feel the energy of the city. But by the time I got to my office at the Nationalities Service Center, I was completely exhausted. All I could do was sit at my desk long enough to gather the strength to get back home.

I rested as much as possible until the end of the month, then began working with "Green Circle" again. Still tiring easily, I could not work two consecutive days, but fortunately, that was not a problem in scheduling with teachers. My assignment that spring took me back to Kensington, this time to St. Anne's, a Catholic elementary school where I was to spend three sessions with every class.

During the first session with a group, I was supposed to tell a story that was intended to help children be accepting of people who are different. Students enjoyed the story, but it didn't touch them personally. So one day in a fourth grade class I told the story of Mumbet instead. The children loved Elizabeth Freeman. They thought she was brave and smart and strong. I asked them why Freeman was mistreated -- was it because of something she did? The children said no, she was mistreated because she was black and she was a slave.

I asked if they had ever been mistreated that way...."not for something you did, but just for who you were?" They looked thoughtful, as though trying to figure that out. Then a girl said: "Yeah, for my name."

"Can you tell us about it?" I asked.

She hesitated, then said that kids teased her because of her last name.

When I asked her how that felt, she hesitated again.

I said, "Remember how courageous Elizabeth Freeman was. Do you think you can be courageous too? Can you tell us how you feel when kids tease you about your name? Would you come up here and stand with me and talk to us?"

Slowly, shyly, Mary Ellen got up and came to the front of the class. I took her hand and asked her to tell us about the teasing. Mary Ellen said her last name was Roche. "I hate it when kids make fun of me for being a bug. It's not spelled the same. My name is R - O - C - H - E." She clung to my hand and looked at me while she talked. "Now look at the class," I said to Mary Ellen. "Tell them how the teasing makes you feel." She squeezed my hand a little tighter, then looked at her classmates and said the teasing hurt her.

"What do you want to ask your classmates?"

"Not to call me that."

"What *do* you want them to call you?"

"Mary Ellen."

Mary Ellen was a chubby girl, shy and unassertive. She had often been the brunt of teasing. Now, for the first time, she was talking about how it made her feel. There was not another sound in the room. All of the children were looking at Mary Ellen. They were attentive and sober.

I thanked Mary Ellen for sharing and for being courageous. Then I asked the children to consider her request. "Who will promise not to call her names?" Most of the hands flew up. A few children hesitated. I told them that no one had to promise, and they shouldn't do it unless they meant it. A few seconds later, the rest of the hands went up. Mary Ellen was beaming. When I went back the following week, she was ecstatic. For seven whole days, no one had called her names.

Others now wanted a turn to share their grievances. Next was a boy who was teased for being fat. Like Mary Ellen, Terry had taken the teasing silently. He came to the front of the room and took my hand. Facing his classmates, he told them how it felt to be called Porky, and how much he hated it. When I asked who would promise to stop teasing Terry, every hand went up.

As we went on talking, one of the girls said she was ugly, which startled everyone in the class. Several children told her how pretty she was, but their words had no effect. Then I asked Beth what she was good at doing. When she couldn't think of an answer, I asked the class to tell me. Someone said Beth was good at math. The teacher nodded, "Yes, she is very good at math."

"Is that true?" I asked Beth. No, she said, she was dumb.

I made a list on the blackboard of all the things people said about Beth. That she was good at riding a bike and playing basketball. That she was generous, helpful, a good friend. Beth loved hearing those things, but she didn't quite believe them. By then, more hands were flying. Other children wanted to hear good things said about them.

At the third session, more children came to the front of the room to hold my hand and talk about things that were hurting them. When I saw that we had about twenty minutes left, I told the children I could tell them a story or we could continue what we were doing, it was their choice. Ordinarily the children would drop anything to hear a story. Now, without a moment's hesitation, they said they wanted to continue what we were doing. With our remaining time together, they got all the sharing and appreciations we could manage.

I was stunned by what low self-esteem these children had. In every classroom I found children who thought themselves dumb or ugly, and could not imagine that their friends thought well of them. I wondered if there was any point in trying to get them to appreciate people of different colors and different cultures. Is it possible to teach children to value other people when they don't value themselves? I put the "Green Circle" script away, and wrote my own as I went along.

In one of the third grades I met Amy, a Puerto Rican child, one of two children in the school who were not white. Her teacher was skeptical about what I was doing.

"What can you accomplish in three sessions?" she asked. I didn't blame her for having doubts; I had them myself. I wasn't sure the program would have any lasting value when there was so little time to work with.

A couple of weeks after I finished with this class, I was walking down the hall when I heard Amy's teacher calling. "Kathy, Kathy!" she said excitedly. "Please come in, I have something to show you." The children in her class kept notebooks for their drawings and stories. The teacher picked up Amy's notebook and opened it to a recent page. "Look," she said, beaming. "Look at the picture Amy drew of herself at the end of your program." I saw a picture of a smiling girl with brown skin.

"Amy has always made herself white," the teacher explained. "This is the first time she has ever drawn herself with brown skin. It's the first time she's had the confidence to feel that it's all right to be herself." The teacher said it was because of my work in her class. It changed the way she viewed the program, and it raised my own hopes. Look what could happen in three sessions!

In one of the sixth grades, when I asked students who were teased for being different to stand next to me, Paul was the first to come up. Because he was short, kids called him Small Paul, and he hated it. There was a girl who was teased for being tall. A boy for being fat. A girl who was teased for wearing braces. Another for not being Catholic. In a few minutes, half the class was in front of the room.

"If we kept on," I asked, "who do you think would be up here?"

"Everyone!" they shouted.

For a moment, no one moved. The children looked around the room at each other. They were taking in the knowledge that all of them felt different in one way or another, and that feeling different gave them something in common.

Toward the end of the session, I asked the students to tell what they liked about other people in the room. The teacher beamed at what the children said about one another. But when I asked them to include the teacher, she looked uncomfortable. She had a reputation for being very strict; I think she wasn't sure she wanted to hear what her students had to say. But they surprised her with accounts of things she had done that they appreciated. That she had given extra help to someone when he was having trouble with math. That a girl had come to school feeling miserable one day, and the teacher's affectionate greeting cheered her up. That she made them feel proud of themselves for doing good work. I asked the teacher if she had ever heard these things before. Her eyes filled with tears and she said no.

I was sorry when my time at St. Anne's was over, but I took a lot with me when I left. I had learned that to help children appreciate others, I had to begin close to home. Helping them appreciate themselves and the people in their lives. Helping them care about kids who are fat or tall or short or wear braces. Perhaps only then would they have a foundation for valuing differences in the larger world.

In the fall, I went back to a Philadelphia associate-superintendent of schools I had become friendly with, and proposed that I teach a course for teachers on multicultural education. She liked the idea and wanted the course to be part of the school district's in-service program which gave teachers the opportunity to earn graduate credits. She called the director of the program and requested that my course be included in the fall curriculum.

The director of the in-service program took it as a criticism of the way the school district was dealing with racial and ethnic tensions. "We're already doing enough," he told me. He was courteous, but never pretended that he welcomed me or the course. "Maybe not enough teachers will sign up," he said, "and it will be cancelled." But within an hour on the first day of registration, 30 teachers enrolled and 12 more were on the waiting list.

I got the course, but everything else seemed to be slipping out of my grasp. First of all, the director of in-service programs would not give approval for me to teach my course again. Secondly, the proposal that David, Linda and I submitted to the school district had languished for more than a year on the superintendent's desk, with no indication that she would ever read it. Without funding, the Multicultural Resource Center would never succeed. It was a year and a half old and still not off the ground. David, Linda and I had to acknowledge that it never would be.

And then I found out that "I Want to Be Free" was no longer on the list of approved materials. I learned about this from a principal who wanted to buy several sets. He was apologetic but said that if it was not listed, he could not place an order. When I called central administration, I spoke with a man who told me that an item has to make sales in order to stay on the list. "But I am making sales," I protested. "Well," came the reply, "then maybe it's because the program has not been updated. Surely you know that material must be revised every few years."

I looked over my original papers of application and approval, and saw nothing about this requirement. Nevertheless, if "I Want to Be Free" was to be reinstated, I had to revise it and submit the program all over again. I couldn't face doing that and I knew it would not make any difference anyway. Going from school to school to make sales wasn't getting me anywhere. With my remaining materials, I gave sets of "I Want to Be Free" to several teachers I knew who wanted them. The last memory I have of my experience with "I Want to Be Free" is of one of the teachers standing on the school steps and hugging the Teacher's Guide as she waved goodbye.

I quit my job doing the Green Circle program, then designed a brochure to promote my services to schools, emphasizing my experience in working with multicultural teaching materials and in helping children appreciate themselves and others. The design looked good, but when I picked up the brochures, I saw that they had been folded wrong. On the next printing, the graphics were washed out. On the third printing the words were blurry.

The manager of the print shop said he had never had such an experience in his life; he could not imagine what was jinxing this job. George thought it was perfectly obvious: this brochure was not meant to be. "For twenty years," he said, "you've been working and struggling in the schools. You've done everything you could, but they will never accept you. This crazy brochure experience is a message. Don't you see? It's time for you to give it up."

George had been the most ardent supporter of my work in the schools. I had a vague suspicion that what he was saying made sense, but I didn't want to hear it. Those brochures gave me a chance to keep my work going. They had become my life line and I was desperately holding on.

Letting Go

With the fourth printing, the brochures finally came out right. I brought them home and spent the rest of the day working on a mailing list and addressing envelopes. I was excited when I went to bed that night, looking forward to the next day when I would put the brochures in the mail.

But when I woke up the following morning, I was so utterly exhausted that I began to sob. In that moment, I knew that I did not have the strength to continue. For five days I looked at the envelopes I had addressed, then I threw them away. I gave away my collection of teaching materials -- pictures, filmstrips, recordings, games, bibliographies, and 200 children's books. I emptied the file cabinet and gave that away too. I saved a few brochures and files, four sets of

"I Want to Be Free" and threw everything else out.

It was 1986. By then, George and I were living together. We had planned to stay in Philadelphia because of my work, but now that I was giving it up, we decided to move to his house in Woodstock, New York.

The hardest part about moving was making a decision about my mother who had been living with us for the past year. With my ongoing fatigue, I could no longer take care of her, so I began taking her for visits to the retirement home we all agreed would be the best one for her. She seemed to like the place, but the day she moved in, my mother was furious. Spitting nails, as the staff said. For two weeks she refused to speak to me. All I could think of was what a terrible daughter I was.

Three weeks later, I had my first anxiety attack. During the following week I had several more. I went to see a therapist. "What does it feel like," she asked, "when you have these attacks?"

"Like I am totally out of control," I answered.

"And what would happen, Kathy, if you let yourself be out of control?"

What an astonishing question! Why, of course, I would die. But Marilyn helped me see that I would not die. Perhaps I could just let go and see what happened. She said I might even get to enjoy feeling out of control because it's a loosening up.

Letting go. The thought was terrifying. But the next day, when I had another anxiety attack, I was determined to try it. As I felt myself being pushed toward a pit of darkness, I imagined spreading my arms and soaring freely into it. I said: it's all right, I don't need to be afraid, I will not die. It's all right, it's all right. As I floated in the darkness, I could hear the words and the music from a Simon and Garfunkel tune: "Hello, darkness, my old friend."

I thought of a quote from Frederick Douglass about people who want crops without turning up the soil and want the ocean without the awful roar of its waters. Those are the people who want change without turmoil. Such a thing is not possible, Douglass said; change comes only with struggle. He was talking about the political and social conditions that breed injustice. But it occurred to me that his words apply to personal, inner change as well.

My anxiety attacks became less intense and gradually disappeared. With my mother settled into her new home and speaking to me again, and Lisa, her husband Michael, and Christie in a rental house nearby, George and I made plans to move.

In Woodstock, we had a simple marriage ceremony performed by the local justice of the peace. Our home became a cozy nest where I had the time and the peace and quiet to begin writing about my recent experiences. With George also writing about personal events, we had wonderful conversations, reading to each other what we had written, discussing, challenging, clarifying.

But it was a mixed blessing. I resented my loss of energy. Sometimes after a short errand, I could do nothing more than go home and go to bed. Driving to Philadelphia had become a nightmare. Normally an easy trip, the first time I went after moving to Woodstock, I was exhausted and gasping for breath by the time I reached the first rest area on the New York Thruway. I spent an hour at each of the remaining rest stops, gathering enough energy to continue. After that, I took the bus to Philadelphia, though it was still an exhausting trip. Everything I did became shaped by what the event was and how much time I would be away.

My doctor had no explanation. It was when I subscribed to a Chronic Fatigue Syndrome journal that I began to feel some relief. Many symptoms of Chronic Fatigue were discussed in the journal, often including stories of people who had the same symptoms that I had. Maybe that did not explain what was happening to me, but it helped to know that I was not alone in what I was experiencing.

Finding Mumbet

When I moved to Woodstock, I took four classroom sets of the "I Want to Be Free" program with me. I put them in the shed, hoping that some day a school would be interested. Two years later, I decided it was never going to happen. I opened the boxes and retrieved the Teachers Guides and copies of *Mumbet: The Story of Elizabeth Freeman* that I wanted to keep. I taped the boxes closed with the rest of the classroom materials inside, and George took them to the dump. As I watched him drive off, I felt relieved. I'd finally let go of that bit of my past.

At the same time, it suddenly hit me: That's where Elizabeth Freeman was buried, and it's not far from Woodstock. How many times had I told her story to children? And I always ended by saying: "If you ever go to

Stockbridge, Massachusetts, you can visit the cemetery and find her grave." Now I was going to do it myself.

When I got to Stockbridge, I went to the public library and asked for help in finding the cemetery. I was sent to the basement where I found two women absorbed in clipping articles for the library files. They seemed to be the town historians, and were delighted to meet someone who knew about Elizabeth Freeman. They told me stories about the family where Mumbet had lived for many years, and told me where to find the house, still occupied by descendants of those early Sedgwicks. Then they directed me to the cemetery and the Sedgwick family plot where Mumbet was buried.

I walked around the cemetery, looked at family markers, then sat on Mumbet's grave and began to talk to her. I said that I had told her story to several hundred school children, and they always loved her. I told Mumbet that she had helped children feel better about themselves and become more respectful of others. When they dramatized her in role-plays or talked about her courage, they began to stand tall and speak in strong voices and find their strength. As I stretched out my legs on her grave and leaned back to enjoy the sun, I felt a bond with Mumbet who had taught me the power of stories.

For it was stories, always the stories, that captured the children's imaginations. From slaves who fought in the American Revolution, to heart-thumping accounts of slaves who escaped to the north, to Canada, or to England. What better stories could there be?

Years later, I would come across an interview of an ex-Klansman, C.P. Ellis, who had once been the Exalted Cyclops of the Durham, North Carolina chapter of the Ku Klux Klan. His story appears in *American Dreams: Lost and Found,* by Studs Terkel, the popular Chicago disc jockey and oral historian.

Ellis said that as a Klansman, he enjoyed the attention he got from influential people in Durham. City councilmen and county commissioners began to call him their friend and occasionally invite C.P to their homes.

But his feelings abruptly changed one day when he was in town and saw a councilman he knew. He walked toward the man to say hello, but the councilman turned his back and crossed the street. It was a transformative moment for C.P. For in a flash, he understood that he was being used. Town leaders called on him to help with actions they wanted to take against the local black residents. C.P. had met with these white men in their homes and talked with them on their phones, but he was not part of their social standing in the community, and never would be. They would not even recognize him in public.

C.P. left the Klan, but said he still hated black people. He eventually became part of a committee that was charged with figuring out how to solve racial problems in the schools that his children attended. C.P. had offered to take part, but he was horrified to learn that he was assigned to work with a black woman. She didn't look forward to working with him, either, but they agreed to do their best. One day, as the two of them began to talk, they discovered that their children were having similar problems in school. Seeing that they had things in common, they listened eagerly to one another's stories, and from there, went on to develop a warm friendship. After that, the world opened up for C.P. He went back to school to get an eighth grade education and eventually a high school diploma. Years later, he began listening to tapes of Martin Luther King. "I listen," he said, "and tears come to my eyes 'cause I know what he's sayin' now. I know what's happenin'."

I often think of the children I worked with at St. Anne's. Did Mary Ellen grow in self confidence? Does Amy continue to feel comfortable in her brown skin? Is Paul no longer teased for being short? I'll never know what happened to them, and so I was particularly moved to learn about C.P Ellis, whose life bears witness to the possibility of lasting change. Storytellers say that stories can save the world. C.P. Ellis might have agreed.

Coming Back

In 1993, after seven years in Woodstock, George and I began to talk about leaving. I was longing to be closer to my children and grandchildren; I wanted to be part of their lives, not an occasional guest. And George's health was precarious; it frightened me to think that I might have to care for him where we had only a small circle of friends and no easy access to specialized medical facilities.

The move was surprisingly easy. A friend bought our house in Woodstock and we found one in the Mt. Airy neighborhood area of Philadelphia, half a mile from Lisa, her husband and two young boys, and a few miles from Christie. Lisa was a nurse practitioner by then. Christie was a hairdresser and working on a degree in art history at Temple University. Soon after George and I were settled, she began to visit us regularly, initiating good conversations by asking for our thoughts about the latest paper she was writing.

This part of the city was perfect for us. Mount Airy has been a racially mixed community for many years, one of the few in the country that have been successful. It is full of writers, artists, and people active in numerous causes. We loved the diversity and felt right at home. Our house was half a block from a small woods and a few minutes' drive from the Wissahickon Valley, a wooded park that runs for five miles along a creek and has many trails for biking and walking.

A few weeks after we moved, I noticed a small announcement in the local paper about a gathering at Fran's Multicultural Resource Center. I could hardly believe my eyes -- the name sounded just like the center that David, Linda, and I had tried to start nine years earlier, and it was only a few blocks from my house. I had to go. When I arrived, I found myself in the living room of a large home, surrounded by books on display. Books for young people, portraying all ethnic groups, like the collection I had had, only larger. I saw that I was among a diverse group of people, which made me feel at home.

Fran gave a short talk about the Multicultural Resource Center and what she hoped to accomplish. She was a tall, handsome African American woman about my age, newly retired from the School District of Philadelphia where she had worked for many years, 18 of them as a high school principal. As she spoke, I was transported back in time. She had the same passion for her work that I had had, the same conviction about the need to have resources for children that did not portray a lily-white world. It could have been me giving that talk.

After the program, I introduced myself. "I once started a center like this," I said, "I even gave it the same name." Fran asked if I had lived on Cedar Avenue. "Yes," I replied, "how did you know?" She said, "When I went to get incorporated, they told me I couldn't call this place the Multicultural Resource Center because someone already had that name. So I became *Fran's* Multicultural Resource Center." She laughed, threw her arms around me and said, "So *you're* the one who kept me from getting the name I wanted!" She had incorporated in August when George and I were moving to Woodstock. She found my name and tried to get in touch with me but couldn't get a forwarding address, so she said to herself, "I'll never meet that woman." And now there I was in her living room.

Fran's center had the things I never had: connections, a financial base, and a physical location. Here was the opportunity I pined for ten years earlier, now at my doorstep. Fran invited me to work with her but with continuing limits to my energy, I couldn't do it. Fate seemed to be playing a cruel joke, dangling something in front of me that I had wanted so badly, and now it was too late. All I could do was to be part of a supportive group of people for Fran, and begin the legal process of dissolving my old corporation so she could have the name she wanted.

While I was wistful about not being able to be involved with the Multicultural Resource Center, it soon became clear that I needed my energy for other things. First, for dealing with breast cancer, then for the caregiving that was required as George's health declined over the next ten years until his death in 2005.

The Last Dream

I've had many frustrations and sorrows about all the roadblocks I had faced, all the times I had thought "if only..." I needed to let go of all of that and hold on to memories of the excitement I so often felt during my years in the schools. I was privileged to have had work that I felt passionate about. And, in spite of concerns about what it meant for my parenting, I've had the joy of seeing my daughters grow up to be kind, loving, wise women with passions of their own.

It has been a long journey, bumpy and wondrous, painful and beautiful, that I trace back to the summer in Texas when I was nine, and my heart ached for the things I saw for which there were no good answers. My most vivid memory is of the woman in the gazebo, the dark-skinned woman they called Lackey, old and worn, bent silently over her work. A person thrown away, it seemed to me, and I wanted to change the world where such a thing can happen.

From time to time, I dreamed about the gazebo. Always in my dream I was a child, standing on the circle drive, looking at Lackey and longing to set her free. Over the years, the dream changed. Instead of being rooted to the ground, unable to do anything, I began to see myself talking to Lackey or trying to open the door to the gazebo. And she began to see me, would even smile. In another dream, I opened the door and Lackey stepped out. Then I turned and bowed to a cheering audience. I was standing on a stage, in front of the curtain. I smiled as everyone applauded, but I knew it wasn't the end of the story.

The next dream was the last one and the best one. In this dream, Lackey opened the door herself, flinging it wide, stepping out and standing tall. We embraced one another, she who had been inside the cage and I who had been on the outside. Then we laughed, grabbed our suitcases and ran away, hand in hand. As I watched the two figures disappear in the distance, it became harder and harder to tell where one ended and the other began.

Eighty years have passed since that time in Goliad when I first saw Lackey and the gazebo. They are gone now, but the hanging tree is still there, spreading its branches and casting a shadow over the town square. I suppose I still live in that shadow, for there is no end to the hatred, cruelty and racial violence that make me want to weep. But I have also seen the possibilities for change, and I hold on to the hope they give. I also hold on to the hope that I see in the last dream, for it reminds me that people have the capacity to reach across the things that divide us, to join hands, and even to run away together.

Acknowledgements

I appreciate the following letters more than I can say, but "I Want to Be Free" would never have been the success that it was without the principals and teachers who welcomed me so warmly into their schools and classrooms. They are the ones who brought my program to life and, for that, I will be forever grateful.

PHILIP H. SHERIDAN PUBLIC SCHOOL
ONTARIO AND G STREETS
PHIADELPHIA, PA 19134

May 20, 1982

I taught I WANT TO BE FREE in 1978 when it was being field tested and again in 1980 after testing had been completed.

My fifth/sixth grade classes were composed of children who had had reading difficulties in school. Most of them were white, all from working class families. Initially, I thought I would have to rewrite some of the materials in an easier reading level. However, the children's interest was so high that they handled the reading without change. They participated easily in all of the activities and were excited about what they were learning. Their discussions and questions revealed the extent of their involvement and the growth that was taking place. Their knowledge was expanded as well as their understanding of other people and their awareness of injustice.

Some of these benefits were passed on to their parents when I made a point of involving them in the program. Students shared the materials with family members, several mothers went with us to the Afro-American History Museum and helped with preparations for the school assembly that we presented as the culminating experience for I WANT TO BE FREE. Every class in the school attended the program, as well as many parents and a number of teachers from other schools.

There was a great deal of excitement among students, faculty and parents about the publicity that was given the school because of I WANT TO BE FREE. A local newspaper columnist wrote a glowing account of the school's involvement with the program, and a television station filmed the assembly program and included a small portion of it on the evening news.

As a result of using I WANT TO BE FREE, the attitudes of my white students changed dramatically. They wanted to learn more about black people in history, and to help design a voluntary desegregation plan for their school. They became increasingly aware of bigotry that they experienced outside of school, and conscious of the need for social conditions to change. Working with parents and teachers, they helped plan and implement an exchange program with an all-black school in another part of the city. Thirty students from each school participated in this highly successful two-week exchange.

I am impressed with the integrated nature of I WANT TO BE FREE. It is really a multi-ethnic approach when recognition is made of the extra reading the children did. The interest was high because the students could relate the content to their own experiences.

The high interest also enabled the students to see the value of reading and writing. Many of my students improved in their basic skills during the years that we used I WANT TOBE FREE. In 1980 the entire class was involved in a city-wide essay writing contest in reference to black history. Of the nine students selected to make live presentations, one was a student of mine who had been considered academically deficient. It was the I WANT TO BE FREE program that stimulated her cultural awareness and motivated her to challenge and do independent research.

I am excited about the numerous ways I WANT TO BE FREE enriches my curriculum. I will continue to use the program.

(signed)

Laree P. Owens

PHILIP H. SHERIDAN SCHOOL
ONTARIO AND G STREETS
PHILADELPHIA, PA. 19134

May 20, 1982

I taught the I WANT TO BE FREE program in the spring of 1980. I had a fifth grade class; all but three or four of my students were white. Their concepts about blacks were amazing. These white students did not realize that blacks were in slavery or that blacks could read or think. They had many misconceptions. For example, they thought it was all right to call a black person nigger, but that it would make a black person angry – even dangerous – to be called black. The parents of these white children had the same misconceptions and stereotypes. I WANT TO BE FREE helped change attitudes. The white children became more knowledgeable about black people and much more accepting. The black students, who stayed to themselves when first coming to the school, began to mix with the white students.

I WANT TO BE FREE had other benefits. The use of basic skills fit into my overall program, worked into the pupil competencies I was developing. I also found the sequence of events in I WANT TO BE FREE valuable. The material helped children understand sequential order.

Children were able to relate things they learned in I WANT TO BE FREE to other learning experiences. One of these was the televised version of Roots, which they loved. I WANT TO BE FREE deepened their understanding of the events taking place. Also, about that time, my students read a play about Susan B. Anthony. I WANT TO BE FREE helped them analyze the status of women compared with the status of black people.

I WANT TO BE FREE was used for our social studies for one-fourth of the school year, and also related in valuable ways to other parts of the overall curriculum.

(signed)
James A. Strong

PHILIP H. SHERIDAN SCHOOL
ONTARIO AND G STREETS
PHILADELPHIA, PA 19134

May 20, 1982

I taught I WANT TO BE FREE during the spring of 1980 to my sixth grade. The students had heard of slavery, but did not know what it meant. They were surprised by the story of <u>Mumbet</u> because they had no idea that people's rights were taken away. My white students didn't really know about discrimination. The I WANT TO BE FREE program expanded their knowledge and opened their minds and hearts to social conditions around them. It did so in a way that captured their enthusiasm, drew black students and white students together in shared concern for the issues they were studying.

The use of basic skills and the variety of activities – including ones that were optional –made I WANT TO BE FREE easy to integrate into other areas of the sixth-grade curriculum.

(signed)
Thomas A. Nally

PHILIP H. SHERIDAN SCHOOL
ONTARIO AND G STREETS
PHILADELPHIA, PA. 19134

June 17, 1982

I taught I WANT TO BE FREE to my sixth grade students for one marking period in the spring of 1980. One of the most valuable results of the program was its reinforcements of concepts of individual rights and freedom. Children grew in their appreciation that everyone wants to be free, wants to be treated as a human being. It helped my students , realize the terrible consequences of slavery. It helped them understand that there is no need to feel guilty, but that we are responsible for our actions – and that includes all forms of bigotry and injustice that are a continuing legacy of a system of slavery based on color.

Young people in an integrated setting can see for themselves what is true. The value of I WANT TO BE FREE is that it gives young people an integrated experience that strongly combats what is taught elsewhere. It creates a strong carry-over effect because when children can begin to see one "strange" group of people as fully human, then barriers are broken to other groups as well. It is an essential part of education.

When I first taught I WANT TO BE FREE, most of my students were white. Our school is in a poor working class community. I WANT TO BE FREE helped my students break through barriers of fear and misunderstanding.

With I WANT TO BE FREE, my students also loved history – the biography, role playing and other activities made history come alive for them; they could identify with the people and the problems presented in the program.

Good integration of basic skills added to the value of I WANT TO BE FREE. I enjoyed teaching the program because it was interesting and it enhanced the overall curriculum.

(signed)
Raymond Franzen

PHILIP H. SHERIDAN SCHOOL
ONTARIO AND G STREETS
PHILADELPHIA, PA. 19134

April 6, 1982

Sheridan School participated in the field testing of I WANT TO BE FREE in 1978. In 1980 the Home and School Association purchased four sets of the completed program which was taught in the two fifth grades and two sixth grades for one marking period in the spring of that year.

The I WANT TO BE FREE program had great impact on the students' attitudes. It required to them to deal with problems today and the impact of black/white relations.

The program is excellently organized and easily implemented as a supplement, or integrated into the existing program. It is flexible, lending itself to reading and speaking skills. The play that was done here at Sheridan School by the fifth and sixth grades was a wonderful way to tie it all together, for the play highlighted a variety of student skills in addition to presenting specific parts of I WANT TO BE FREE.

Intergroup education and the role of Afro-Americans in history are mandated parts of our curriculum. This is an exciting way to answer that mandate. I'd like to see teachers at Sheridan continue to use I WANT TO BE FREE. I'd like to have my own children use it. Because the program was successful here in a white working class community, it can probably be successful in just about any setting. I hope it will become known to teachers in other parts of the city.

(signed)
Marshall Gorodetzer, Principal

Made in the USA
Middletown, DE
11 July 2020